BRITISH Sports Cars
Road Tests

BRITISH Sports Cars Road Tests

Nigel Fryatt

Autocar

Hamlyn · London · New York · Sydney · Toronto

Most of the illustrations in this book are from the
archives of *Autocar*; for additional material the
publishers are grateful to Neill Bruce Photographic,
Peter Cramer and The National Motor Museum

Published by The Hamlyn Publishing Group Limited
London · New York · Sydney · Toronto
Astronaut House, Feltham, Middlesex, England

© Copyright IPC Business Press Limited 1982

ISBN 0 600 34977 2

All rights reserved. No part of this publication may
be reproduced, stored in a retrieval system, or transmitted,
in any form or by any means, electronic, mechanical,
photocopying, recording or otherwise, without the
permission of The Hamlyn Publishing Group
and the copyrightholder

Printed in Italy

Contents

Introduction	*6*
MG Midget TC	*8*
Jaguar XK120	*14*
Triumph TR2	*20*
MG MGA	*26*
Austin-Healey Sprite	*32*
AC Ace	*38*
Austin-Healey 3000	*44*
Daimler SP250	*50*
Aston Martin DB4	*56*
Sunbeam Tiger 260	*62*
MG MGB GT	*68*
Lotus Elan S4	*74*
Lotus Seven Twin Cam SS	*80*
Jensen-Healey	*86*
Reliant Scimitar GTE	*92*
Jaguar E-type V12	*98*
Morgan Plus 8	*104*
Triumph TR7 Drophead	*110*
TVR Tasmin	*116*
Lotus Esprit Turbo	*122*

Introduction

There is a fine tradition in Great Britain for building sports cars. This became apparent when deciding which twenty cars should be included in this book. The final selection spans a 35 year period of vastly changing attitudes and styles. They are all of special significance, with shapes and performance that vary enormously. With technological advance, engineering ideas admired when they were introduced are now often commonplace and taken for granted by the modern driver, while in some cases their performance is impressive only in perspective.

The purpose of this book is to show the development of the British sports car, since 1945, through twenty road tests carried out by *Autocar*. The original tests have been edited, but they still retain the flavour of the attitudes and styles of the period in which they were written. Time has naturally made some remarks obsolete. The enthusiasm that *Autocar* testers had for these cars must always be considered in relation to the period in which they were written. For instance, the impression made by the Jaguar XK120 in 1950 can be quantified when it is realised that the car's acceleration is comparable today with a Vauxhall Cavalier or a Talbot Solara – this in no way diminishes the importance of the Jaguar, it merely is a point to bear in mind when reading the earlier tests. Each test is prefaced by a short introduction to explain

The Mk II version of the Austin-Healey 3000

The Lotus Turbo Esprit

the car's significance, and a summary at the end outlines the history of the car since the time of the test.

When comparing the oldest representative with the most recent – the MG TC and the Lotus Esprit Turbo – it will be seen that both represent the archetypal sports car of their respective periods. The MG with its upright radiator, separate wings and headlights, appealed to young people everywhere, but what is more important in terms of its success, it appealed to Americans, and began the tradition of exporting British sports cars to the United States. The Lotus Esprit is a perfect example of the sports car tradition of transferring the knowledge gained at the race track to everyday use on the road. It represents the style of the 1980s with its low, sleek body and turbocharged engine amidships.

What have these two cars got in common? They are both able to offer performance and handling qualities that add up to a style of motoring that raises them above their respective contemporaries. There can be no doubt – the MG TC and the Lotus Esprit Turbo are both *sports* cars.

The remaining cars tested have similar qualities. While body shapes may change, aerodynamic trends and production developments have caused many changes in sports car design. The earlier metal panelled bodies bolted to separate chassis gave way to the pressed steel monocoque construction of the MGB. Development of glassfibre body mouldings have played an important part in the shape of the TVR Tasmin and the Lotus Esprit. Racing experience of suspension and chassis design has brought about improvements in handling. The AC Ace was Britain's first sports car with independent suspension on all four wheels; the Lotus Elan adapted a backbone chassis and a simple but very effective suspension system.

Is the age of the sports car dead? No. Of the twenty cars tested in the book, five are still in production. Two, the Morgan Plus 8 and the Lotus Seven (now built as the Caterham Seven) are throwbacks to an earlier age, fervently refusing to bend to modern day conventions – and are still in great demand. The other three, the Reliant Scimitar GTC, TVR Tasmin and the Lotus Esprit Turbo are very much the modern sports car – they even have luxury fittings like electric windows!

Unfortunately the days of the cheap, low-cost sports car are definitely over. Today, British manufacturers do not have, or do not wish to find, the money to include a sports car within their model range. They tell us it does not make economic sense – not even using stock parts to keep down the costs – a practice that brought about the Austin-Healey Sprite. This sad fact was never better underlined than by the 1981 closure, by BL, of the MG factory at Abingdon.

The enthusiasm that this form of motoring generates, however, will mean that the sports car will always remain. The cars featured in this book have all become 'classics' in their own right. And as new models appear they too will come under *Autocar*'s close road test scrutiny to ensure that they are upholding the Great British sports car tradition.

I am indebted to past and present colleagues of the staff of *Autocar* who painstakingly carried out the original road tests on which this book is based.

NF

MG Midget TC

Cycle wings and wire wheels, the style of the late 1940s that still look good today

When MG returned to car manufacture after the Second World War, their need for quick sales, especially export sales, led to the decision to revive a proven design. The MG TC Midget was based on the pre-war TB type (of which only 379 had been made).

The TC had a ladder-style channel section chassis frame with tubular cross members, and a separate wood-framed body with steel panelling for the two-seater body. It was powered by a four-cylinder cast-iron 1,250 cc engine, with twin horizontal SU carburettors, developing 54 bhp at 5,200 rpm.

Production began in 1945 although *The Autocar* did not road test one until late 1947, and was quick to point out that, at a time when there was much talk about rationalization, and when more and more cars tended to resemble one another in both appearance and performance, the MG TC Midget stood unique.

The austerity of the immediate post-war years was lightened a little by what in 1947 was said to be a 'real' car – upright radiator, separate wings and headlamps and small cutaway doors. The TC was cheap enough to appeal to many young people (the basic price was £375 in 1945, rising to £412 from mid-1946) and was much liked by American GIs returning home. The TC

The original *Autocar* road test car in contemporary surroundings

The 1,250 cc engine was easy to maintain and produced 54·4 bhp

was the antipathy of the then accepted American breed of motor car and thus a strong export market began, boosted by cheap initial cost and moderate running costs.

By present day standards the TC's performance might not seem particularly fast – 0 to 60 mph in 22·7 sec – but liberal use of the gearbox led to *The Autocar* describing progress in a TC as being 'vivid'. The TC was no more difficult to drive than any of the ordinary saloons of the period, the 1,250 cc engine being quite flexible in top gear and thus the car was very tractable in traffic. With an engine that was happy to rev freely without complaint, much could be made of the performance with 40 mph possible in second, 60 mph in third, and a top speed in fourth of 75 mph.

The handy size of the vehicle complemented its ability to pass safely where bigger cars might have been held up by much slower moving traffic, cross-country

The windscreen is shown folded down, with the 'racing' screens in place

progress found the TC as fast a car as any on the roads at that time. The responsive steering and praised cornering ability were big factors that accounted for high average speed capabilities without an extremely high maximum speed. The TC was tested over a variety of different road conditions, through crowded towns as well as cross country journeys and attained an average speed of around 44–46 mph.

Drivers spoke of the complete sense of command felt over the car at all times, the car responded readily to the controls, and felt eager. Steering and road-holding were complimented with particular praise going to the Lockheed drum brakes.

At this time there was much discussion about the effectiveness of 'normal' versus independent suspension. The TC was fitted with 'normal' suspension – that is, a solid beam front axle with half-elliptic leaf springs with a live rear axle and half-elliptic springs. Good handling characteristics were, therefore, matched with something of harsh ride over poor surfaces.

This trim and appealing little car was practically laid out and offered good accessibility for ease of maintenance, which backed an affection for the car's efficiency and willingness. This practical vehicle offered fresh-air style of progress, but also had good all-weather equipment. The hood was easily erected, the side screens likewise, making the TC quite reasonable for bad weather use.

The driving position allowed for adjustment for the seat back rest and the spring-spoked steering wheel was telescopically adjustable. A feature that was either liked or disliked at the time was the fly-off handbrake – in *The Autocar*'s view it was thought a form of control to be highly commended for its certainty and ease of operation.

GENERAL SPECIFICATION

Engine
Head/block	cast iron
Cylinders	4 in line
Bore/stroke	66·5 × 90 mm
Capacity	1,250 cc
Cooling	water
Valve gear	overhead pushrod
Compression	7·25:1
Carburettor	twin SU
Max. power	54·4 bhp at 5,200 rpm
Max. torque	64 lb-ft at 2,600 rpm

Transmission
Type	4-speed manual
Gear ratios	
Top	1·000:1
3rd	1·352:1
2nd	1·951:1
1st	3·379:1
Final drive	5·125:1

Suspension
Front	beam front axle with half-elliptic leaf springs
Rear	live axle by half-elliptic leaf springs

Steering
Type	Bishop cam and lever
Assistance	no

Brakes
Front	Lockheed 9-in drum
Rear	Lockheed 9-in drum
Servo	no

Wheels
Type	knock-off wire
Tyres	4·5-19 in

Electrical
Battery	12v, 51 a-h
Earth	positive
Dynamo	Lucas C45YV
Headlamps	36/36W (left hand); 36W (right hand)

The gearchange had syncromesh on second, third and top and with a short vertical lever, quick upward and downward changes could be made, enabling maximum performance to be got from the car. The instruments included a rev-counter directly in front of the driver, with the speedometer directly in front of the passenger!

The headlamps were thought to be good for fast night driving. Starting from cold was immediate, and not much use was needed of the choke on the twin SU carburettors before the engine would pull properly. A much praised point on the TC was the big fuel tank that gave a possible range of 400 miles between fill ups.

The impact of the MG TC in America was enormous, and the car spearheaded British export sales abroad – of the 10,000 TCs ever made, nearly one third were exported, (in terms of numbers, the TC was MG's 'best ever' at that time).

The TC gave way to the TD in 1949, which was distinguished by a box-section chassis, coil spring independent suspension and rack and pinion steering. In the autumn of 1953, the TD was replaced by the 1,466 cc-engined TF which only two years later gave way to an entirely new type of MG sports car, the MGA, in 1955 (see page 26).

The driver faces the rev-counter, the passenger the speedometer!

PERFORMANCE DATA
Date of test 17th October 1947

Maximum speeds		*mph*
Top		75
3rd		61
2nd		40
1st		25

Acceleration from rest	
mph	*sec*
0–30	5·7
0–50	14·7
0–60	22·7

Acceleration in	**top**	**3rd**
mph	*sec*	*sec*
10–30	12·1	8·9
20–40	13·5	9·5
30–50	14·9	10·3

Fuel consumption
Overall	31 mpg
Tank capacity	13·5 gal.
Max. range	418 miles

Jaguar XK120

The Jaguar XK120 has a claim to have been *the* major sports car of the 1950s, and certainly it had a great influence on sports car design. The car itself came about almost incidentally, built as a 'limited edition' batch of sports cars with an aluminium body to publicize Jaguar's new saloon car engine. The response from the XK120's first public appearance at the 1948 Earls Court Motor Show in London was such that Jaguar decided to go into production and build the car with a steel body.

The engine concerned was the first mass-produced twin-cam unit originally designed for the Mk VIII saloon but was ready for production two years before the saloon. This remarkable straight-six 3,442 cc engine, which was to become the mainstay of the Jaguar range, was fitted to a box-section chassis, with independent front suspension using torsion bar springs with a live rear axle suspended on leaf springs at the rear. The model's 120 designation referred to its claimed 120 mph top speed — a claim which made a great impression at the car's launch and was later to be underlined when the XK120 was timed along the famous Jabbeke Road in Belgium. Fitted with an undershield and a racing type windscreen (both items available as optional equipment for road versions) the car achieved 132·6 mph over a flying mile and 126 mph with the normal windscreen and hood and side screens erected, thus for its time the XK120 was indisputably the fastest series production car in the world.

Nothing like the XK120 had ever been achieved, especially at that price (£1,263 in 1950). It was a car with tremendous performance and yet it displayed the flexibility, and even the silkiness and smoothness, of a mild-mannered saloon.

The heart of this astonishing versatility was the $3\frac{1}{2}$-litre engine that developed 160 bhp at 5,100 rpm with impressive smoothness, and maintained that figure on a flat peak of the power curve towards the 6,000 rpm mark. The car we tested was the first steel-bodied production model, and despite some enthusiastic treatment the new engine showed no sign of losing tune, used little oil and did not at any time record

The flush-sided body with closed-in rear wheel was well ahead of its time

The first *Autocar* test car was a left-hand drive version, destined for America

a water temperature above 80 deg C throughout the test.

The XK120 had a dual character. It could be handled quietly with little use of the gears if the driver was in a lazy mood. Press the right foot hard down, however, and a different car was revealed. For its time, the ability to reach a very high speed – 0–100 mph in 35·5 sec – was thought to be phenomenally quick. The top gear acceleration also emphasized the engine's flexibility (our test car had an overall top gear ratio of 3·64:1; there were several optional rear-axle ratios).

Even town driving was thought a pleasure in this car, with the driver able to nip in and out of traffic swiftly, while at the other extreme the XK could be hurled round bends with confidence. The steering was light and high geared with sufficient castor action to allow good response. Well-damped suspension, telescopic dampers at

The soft top was not the most flattering part of the car's design

the front with dampers and half-elliptic springs at the rear, with normal tyre pressures produced a ride that was considered to be every way comparable with the best independently sprung car of the day.

The Lockheed hydraulically operated drum brakes had special linings to prevent fade. The central gear lever was placed rather too far back – close to the driver – than some testers would have liked. There was synchromesh on second, third and top, and third gear was particularly quiet and could be sustained for long periods of alternative acceleration and deceleration on a winding road.

The production model we tested was a

GENERAL SPECIFICATION

Engine
Head/block	cast iron
Cylinders	6 in line
Bore/stroke	83 × 106 mm
Capacity	3,442 cc
Cooling	water
Valve gear	twin ohc
Compression	8:1
Carburettor	twin SU
Max. power	160 bhp at 5,100 rpm
Max. torque	195 lb-ft at 2,500 rpm

Transmission
Type	4-speed manual
Gear ratios	
Top	1·000:1
3rd	1·367:1
2nd	1·982:1
1st	3·375:1
Final drive	3·64:1

Suspension
Front	independent by wishbones, torsion bars, anti-roll bar
Rear	Half-elliptic springs

Steering
Type	Burman recirculatory ball
Assistance	no

Brakes
Front	Lockheed 12-in drum
Rear	Lockheed 12-in drum
Servo	no

Wheels
Type	centre-lock wire
Tyres	6·00–16 in

Electrical
Battery	12v, 64 a-h
Earth	positive
Dynamo	Lucas C45PVS
Headlamps	48/48W

left-hand drive version destined for the USA, and had a high compression ratio intended for the higher octane fuel it was to encounter, but even with lower octane fuel only slight pinking was experienced.

Inside the XK120 there was just sufficient elbow room, with adjustable front seats upholstered in good quality leather, which gave a very upright driving position, but nevertheless had adequate support for the shoulders. In front of the driver the instruments were set in the centre of the facia, with the rev counter on the left and the 140 mph speedometer on the far right – facing the passenger! Oil pressure and water temperature gauges were also on the leather covered facia. The door catches were operated by leather pulls and the doors could be locked from the inside, which was unusual for an open car of this period.

Accessibility to the engine was particularly good, with the sparking plugs mounted in the well between the two 70 degree camshaft covers, with the oil filter placed in the left camshaft cover.

In 1950 our enthusiasm for the XK120 was unbounded. It perpetuated Jaguar's reputation for outstanding value-for-money performance cars. With hindsight, it was rather naive of Jaguar to think they could introduce this car and restrict it to a limited edition of only 200 aluminium panelled over ash frames models, eventual sales of the pressed-steel produced bodies topped 12,000 in open, drophead coupe and hard top forms.

The 120's successor, in 1954, was the XK140 with its wider body (allowing more cockpit room), revised suspension and uprated engine now producing 190 bhp and with a top speed of just under 120 mph. Three years later the heavier XK150 was introduced. Looking a little more sedate than the original XK, the performance trait was kept when, in 1958, the 'S' version was produced offering 250 bhp and a year later even this was improved when the engine was increased to 3·8 litres and 265 bhp was made available. Performance, therefore, was not to be sacrificed for room and comfort.

The 150 emphasized, however, the XK's transformation from a sports car to a GT, especially when disc brakes and a Borg Warner automatic transmission were made available. Production of the XK150 lasted until 1961, and the replacement for it was as sensational as the XK120 had been 13 years before (see page 98).

PERFORMANCE DATA
Date of test 14th April 1950

Maximum speeds	mph
Top	115
3rd	76
2nd	54
1st	28

Acceleration from rest	
mph	sec
0–30	4·0
0–50	8·3
0–60	12·0
0–70	15·5
0–80	19·0
0–90	25·9
0–100	35·3

Acceleration in	top	3rd
mph	sec	sec
10–30	7·8	5·6
20–40	7·5	5·4
30–50	7·8	5·9

Fuel consumption	
Overall	15 mpg
Tank capacity	15 gal.
Max. range	225 miles

Opposite, top: The XK120 was a practical sports car with a useful boot

Opposite, bottom: The neat interior, with leather-covered facia and fly-off handbrake

Above: The versatile twin-overhead camshaft six-cylinder engine was to power many future Jaguars

Triumph TR2

Post-war production of the Triumph Division of the Standard Motor Company consisted initially of two versions of the Triumph 1800, a knife-edge saloon and a roadster, both cars were able to seat up to five, although in the roadster two people were carried in occasional seats in the luggage locker. Later, 2-litre units, similar to the Standard Vanguard engine, were fitted to both models. The roadster was a car of sporting character with many of the refinements associated with a drophead coupe, but it was not an out-and-out sports car. A new low-budget programme at Triumph resulted in the TR2, unveiled at the 1952 London Motor Show, although it was not put into production until the following summer.

The idea of the early TR was to produce a simple sports car with low construction and running costs. The result was a robust, rather than elegant, sports car aimed at enthusiastic and often youthful drivers, who wanted a car with performance but did not necessarily have the money to buy an expensive small-series production model.

In the TR, costs were kept down by using existing components; the engine was from the Standard Vanguard (linered down to just below 2 litres), the gearbox and rear axle were from the same car, and the front suspension came from the Triumph Mayflower.

The TR2's performance was demonstrated by runs down the Jabbeke Road in Belgium. In 'speed trim' – with undershield and metal cockpit cover – Ken Richardson, who was responsible for most of the development work, took the car to a top speed of 124 mph for the flying mile. When we tested the road version we achieved a mean top speed of 103 mph with the hood and sidescreens up, and 99 mph in open trim. At the time, *very* few cars could reach a speed of over 100 mph in standard trim and register an overall fuel consumption of 32 mpg, and all at a basic price of £600 (£844 including Purchase Tax).

While it was based on the familiar Vanguard unit, the engine had a capacity of

The zip-fastened openings at the front of the sidescreens allowed the flaps to be clipped in position from inside the car

The recessed radiator grille gave the TR2 a distinctive frontal appearance

1,991 cc, a higher compression ratio, a different camshaft with modified valve gear, and twin SU carburettors, to give 90 bhp at 4,800 rpm in the TR2. The engine was reasonably smooth, with good throttle response.

The model we tested had the optional Laycock-de Normanville overdrive unit fitted to top gear. The clutch operation was smooth and well able to stand fast gear changes without undue slip. The centrally positioned short gear lever had a robust mechanism well able to cope with full throttle changes, with synchromesh on top, third and second gears. The electrically operated overdrive switch was conveniently placed on the facia, the change up to overdrive being quite smooth with only a slight jerk being noticed on down changes unless the clutch pedal was lightly depressed.

The TR2 had a nicely balanced feel, with sufficiently soft suspension to give a satisfactory ride, yet with little body roll in cornering. Ken Richardson's work resulted in quite acceptable handling – the fact that

The interior was well laid out. The passenger had a useful grab handle above the glove box

the rear end sometimes hopped around a bit in corners was thought to be a 'natural' characteristic of sports cars. The drum brakes responded well to our tests, and the handbrake was fitted with a fly-off type of rachet.

Apart from the boom from the exhaust, the TR2 was reasonably quiet, with little wind noise from the hood and side screens, and the car was free from vibration.

In spite of its overall small dimensions, there was thought to be a surprising amount of space in the cockpit. The seats were adjustable, well-upholstered and gave good support. The pedals were nicely arranged for good heel-and-toe operations, and the headlight dip switch provided a rest for the driver's left foot. The metal-spoked steering wheel allowed good visibility of the rev counter and the speedometer directly in front of the driver, with the oil pressure, water temperature, ammeter and fuel gauges in a centre facia panel. The interior was well trimmed with pockets in both doors and a lockable glove compartment. The hood was made of plastic material and was easily erected and dismantled.

The boot was a reasonable size when remembering the overall dimensions of the car, and there was room for a suitcase behind the seats. A separate compartment below the boot floor and behind the number plate housed the spare wheel.

The TR2 was particularly good value for money, offered performance, fuel economy and was fun to drive, yet only 8,628 were built before a more 'civilised' TR3 was introduced in 1955. The TR3, however, had a much longer run.

Distinguished by a different grille, its engine produced another 5 bhp, while output was further raised to 100 bhp in 1956, and later in that same year it became the first British production car to be fitted with disc brakes. The TR3A followed in 1958, complete with hardtop and outside

Removing the number plate allowed access to the car's spare wheel

GENERAL SPECIFICATION

Engine
Head/block	cast iron, wet liners
Cylinders	4 in line
Bore/stroke	83 × 92 mm
Capacity	1,991 cc
Cooling	water
Valve gear	overhead pushrod
Compression	8·5:1
Carburettor	twin SU H4
Max. power	90 bhp at 4,800 rmp
Max. torque	117 lb-ft at 3,000 rpm

Transmission
Type	4-speed manual, with overdrive on top
Gear ratios	
Overdrive	0·82:1
4th	1·00:1
3rd	1·09:1
2nd	1·64:1
1st	3·38:1
Final drive	3·70:1

Suspension
Front	independent by coil springs, wishbones
Rear	live axle by half-elliptic leaf springs

Steering
Type	Bishop cam and lever
Assistance	no

Brakes
Front	Lockheed 10-in drum
Rear	Lockheed 9-in drum
Servo	no

Wheels
Type	centre-lock wire
Tyres	5·50–15 in

Electrical
Battery	12v, 51 a-h
Earth	positive
Dynamo	Lucas
Headlamps	60/36W

The engine was very accessible for routine servicing

door handles. TR3 production continued until 1961 when over 83,000 had been built.

These early TRs had a lot of competition successes, due to a large extent to the car's rugged character and an engine which would perform unflaggingly under duress. The cars competed in events as diverse as the Alpine Rally, the Tourist Trophy and the Le Mans 24 Hour Race. At one time the TR2 was almost standard equipment for the successful British rally driver.

For some Triumph enthusiasts, the classic TR line ended with the TR3A. The wider, more square-cut TR4 introduced in September 1961 was powered by a 2,138 cc engine. The TR4A announced in March 1965 was a softer-sprung model with independent rear suspension from the Triumph 2000. The body and running gear were carried over for the TR5 produced in 1967 with its fuel injected 2,498 cc six-cylinder engine, with the oft quoted 'last traditional British sports car', the TR6, appearing in 1969. This had a Karmann Ghia designed body, with 120 mph performance and a somewhat harsh ride. Following the TR6, there was a complete break with TR tradition when the TR7 was announced (see page 110), first for America, to be introduced in Great Britain in May 1976, and continuing until 1981.

PERFORMANCE DATA
Date of test 8th January 1954

Maximum speeds

	mph
Top	103·5
3rd	65
2nd	42
1st	22

Acceleration from rest

mph	sec
0–30	3·6
0–50	8·2
0–60	11·9
0–70	15·9
0–80	22·3
0–90	31·5
0–100	51·9

Standing ¼ mile 18·7

Acceleration in

mph	top sec	3rd sec
10–30	9·4	7·1
20–40	9·3	6·7
30–50	9·3	6·6
40–60	9·5	6·9
50–70	10·4	7·8
60–80	11·4	—
70–90	14·5	—

Fuel consumption
Overall   32 mpg
Tank capacity   12·5 gal.
Max. range   400 miles

MG MGA

It may have been a radical change from previous models, but the MGA still remains an attractive design

The MGA was the first of an entirely new breed of corporate MG sports cars. The famous upright MG radiator had gone, and the all-enveloping design that owed much to the MG TD based Le Mans car of 1951 clothed BMC mechanicals. Indeed, the production MGA's road holding, braking and steering characteristics were very similar to the Le Mans car that we had tested earlier in 1955.

The engine was the 1,489 cc unit used in the badge-engineered BMC ZA/ZB Magnette saloon, producing 68 bhp. Starting the car presented no problems. The test car was fitted with an optional radiator blind to aid warm-up (an optional extra that many enthusiasts were to indulge, although even without it the engine soon reached the correct operating temperature). Blipping the throttle produced the then familar MG exhaust note, ensuring that even if the car looked rather different to previous MGs, it at least *sounded* right. Throttle response was good, with 70 mph achieved in 21 seconds from rest.

With a smaller 'racing' screen and tonneau cover fitted, 96 mph was possible, with the hood and sidescreens erected this was increased to 99 mph at 5,500 rpm. The car was well able to cruise all day with the speedometer reading between 90 and 100 mph. Fuel consumption benefited from the body shape, with our test figure of just over 27 mpg representing fast motoring and give-and-take town driving.

There was nothing special about the suspension, which at the front was carried over from the TF. However, the balance of the MGA was almost 50/50, which led the car to have road holding and steering of a very high order. Even with the tyre pressures set for fast driving the ride was not harsh. The car's handling characteristics made fast cornering a joy, wet roads would result in tail out oversteer, but this was easily corrected. The car's handling was superior to its rivals, with the car's

scuttle braced chassis being stiff and safe.

Control was helped by the car's excellent driving position. The seat was very low, and was adjustable to allow the driver to position his legs correctly for the pedals, which were well-spaced with enough room around them for those with large feet! The short remote gear lever fell immediately to hand, and its movement was satisfyingly precise, although there was occasional difficulty when trying to select first gear from rest. The hydraulically-operated clutch enabled fast gear changes to be made without slip.

The MGA's braking was based on past racing experience, and the drum brakes showed no sign of fade throughout the test. The centre-lock wire wheels (an option on the MGA) helped to assist cooling of the car's drums, as well as improving the overall appearance of the car. The handbrake lever was to the side of the propellor shaft and had a fly-off action.

Both seats had adequate adjustment, with the backrest set at a comfortable angle. More support around the thighs was thought preferable. On the passenger side a grab handle doubled as a windscreen support.

It was easier for two people to erect the car's hood from its stowed position behind the seats, than for the driver to do so alone. The sidescreens were simple to position and had spring-loaded bottom flaps. At speed there was a little vibration noise from the whole ensemble.

There were no door handles, entry being made by opening the flap in the side screens and pulling on the door handle cord slung across the inside of the door pocket. The release handle for the boot was behind the passenger's seat, and although the boot was occupied by the spare wheel it was still possible to carry a reasonable amount of luggage for a car of this type.

There was no glove compartment in the facia. The test car was fitted with a radio which was an optional extra; where a radio was not specified, the aperture was blanked off by a plate with the MG motif. A large pocket in each door was sufficient for maps and the usual odds and ends, and it remained dry in the rain, even when the sidescreens were not fitted.

The brilliance of the headlights allowed for fast night driving, but the foot-operated dip switch was placed rather high and difficult to reach – it would have been better placed adjacent to the clutch pedal. There was a rheostat for the instrument lighting, and in one position of the switch, the speedometer alone was illuminated. The only reflection on the windscreen came from the tonneau cover studs, immediately in front of the steering wheel. With the hood up and strong headlight beams, the MGA was thought as comforting to drive at night as it was by day.

The 1,498 cc engine was later increased to 1,588 cc, raising the power output from 68 to 75 bhp

The soft top and side-screens do not add much to the car's looks

With the spare wheel aboard, there was not much room for anything else

A heating and demisting unit, available as an optional extra, was fitted to the test car. It worked satisfactorily, drawing fresh air via a long duct in the engine compartment. On the left-hand side of the radiator, fresh air was ducted to the intakes of the twin SU carburettors. Hot air and engine fumes were cleared by vents on each side of the bonnet.

The MGA built up a good reputation for being a safe and reliable sports car, although it was not tremendously fast. It had a noticeable power deficit compared to the Healeys and the TRs, and 1958 saw the introduction of the Twin Cam version. The

GENERAL SPECIFICATION

Engine
Head/block	cast iron
Cylinders	4 in line
Bore/stroke	73·025 × 89 mm
Capacity	1,489 cc
Cooling	water
Valve gear	overhead pushrod
Compression	8·3:1
Carburettor	twin SU H4
Max. power	68 bhp at 5,500 rpm
Max. torque	77·4 lb-ft at 3,500 rpm

Transmission
Type	4-speed manual
Gear ratios	
Top	1·000:1
3rd	1·374:1
2nd	2·214:1
1st	3·640:1
Final drive	4·300:1

Suspension
Front	independent by coil springs, wishbones
Rear	half-elliptic leaf springs

Steering
Type	rack and pinion
Assistance	no

Brakes
Front	Lockheed 10-in drum
Rear	Lockheed 10-in drum
Servo	no

Wheels
Type	pressed-steel
Tyres	5·60–15 in

Electrical
Battery	12v (2 × 6v), 51 a-h
Earth	positive
Dynamo	Lucas C39PV2
Headlamps	42/36W

The interior was a little sparse and basic

PERFORMANCE DATA
Date of test 23rd September 1955

Maximum speeds		mph
Top		98
3rd		58
2nd		38
1st		20

Acceleration from rest	
mph	sec
0–30	4·9
0–50	11·0
0–60	15·6
0–70	21·4
0–80	32·1
0–90	50·1

Standing ¼ mile 20·2

Acceleration in	top	3rd
mph	sec	sec
10–30	—	8·2
20–40	12·2	8·0
30–50	12·3	8·4
40–60	13·1	9·1
50–70	15·0	10·7
60–80	18·1	—

Fuel consumption
Overall 27 mpg
Tank capacity 10 gal.
Max. range 270 miles

1,588 cc twin cam engine gave 108 bhp and this model had a top speed of over 110 mph, with disc brakes all-round and centre-lock perforated wheels as standard. It could have been thought this model would have a long production run. Unfortunately the MGA Twin Cam was rather expensive, and the engine was very temperamental. Production ceased in 1960 after only 2,111 models had been produced.

In 1959 the MGA 1600 was introduced, with the standard engine bored out to 1,588 cc to give 75 bhp and improved torque, and with disc brakes at the front. The MGA 1600 Mk II appeared in 1961 with the engine further increased to 1,622 cc. The improved aerodynamics of the hard top version meant that it was a genuine 100 mph sports car.

Production of MGAs in their various forms topped the 100,000 barrier in 1962 but sales were dropping in the face of faster competition, especially from Triumph. So once again the remarkable BMC B-Series engine was further bored out to 1,800 cc, while the separate chassis frame was replaced by a pressed-steel unit construction bodyshell and the logical replacement for the MGA, the MGB, was born (see page 68).

Austin-Healey Sprite

The Austin-Healey Sprite was designed as a cheap, small sports car using existing BMC stock components. Costing little more than contemporary saloons, it was to complement its larger Austin-Healey brother, and was welcomed because at the time there was not a quantity-produced true sports car in the 1-litre class, and had not been for many years. While the car's acceleration and top speed at first glance seemed modest, the character, behaviour, and economy of operation combined with the low initial cost to make a very rewarding whole.

The Sprite was powered by the BMC 948 cc A-Series engine with twin SU carburettors and extra strong valve springs, with a number of other modifications made to the valves and the bearings to ensure the unit could cope with the 50 bhp gross output claimed. There was a four-speed gearbox, wishbone front suspension and live rear axle with quarter elliptic springs, and the platform chassis supported the now famous body, its protruding headlights gave the car 'character' and later earned it the nickname 'frog-eye'.

With its low weight (about 1,460 lb), small frontal area and smooth under-floor surface, the Sprite was quite a nippy performer for its engine size. The standing quarter mile figure of 21·7 sec was better than many 1½ litre family saloons of the time, and was only 0·5 sec slower than its MG Magnette stable mate. Similarly the mean maximum speed of 80 mph was good enough to hold off challenges of many larger engined saloons.

As the car was specially intended to provide enjoyable, sporting motoring at low cost, the financial aspects were particularly important. Including Purchase Tax, a

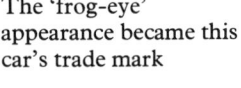
The 'frog-eye' appearance became this car's trade mark

The whole of the bonnet hinged forward to allow access to the A-Series BMC engine

1958 Sprite cost £668 – a very competitive price at the time. To complement this, it had an average fuel consumption of 40 mpg and this and the use of stock BMC parts kept down the costs of service and repairs.

The Sprite was very satisfying on winding roads, where the car's roadholding could be appreciated to the full. With only 2½ turns lock-to-lock, the rack and pinion steering (from the Morris Minor) was very precise – directing the Sprite was all done with the wrists and 'armfuls' of lock were not necessary. The car's structure was very rigid, there being no trace of scuttle shake. The ride was firm to the point of being harsh, but this did not adversely affect roadholding.

The engine would rev easily up to its 6,000 rpm maximum, but the Sprite was not so well served by the gear ratios. First was a natural choice for starting from rest, and while second could be used for the same purpose it would have benefited from higher gearing. The maxima speeds in the gears were 23, 37 and 63 mph. The gap between second and third gear was therefore 26, while the gap between first and second was only 14. A slightly higher first and an appreciably higher second was thought to be necessary – the problem, of course, arose from using stock parts.

A well-placed stubby gear lever permitted fast changes to be made. The synchromesh on the upper three gears coped well with the car's performance and added to the fun of driving this little car. Clutch take-up was just right, for both smooth town driving and fast getaways.

The transmission was quiet, with little sound from either the gearbox or the axle. Naturally the engine itself was a major factor in noise build up, sounding noticeably busy, although compared to its contemporaries not unpleasantly so.

With the hood up there was an appreciable amount of wind roar but when it was

The interior of this low cost sports car was spartan

33

Above: The Sprite was small and compact

Above, right: There was no boot, luggage could be carried behind the seats

down there was much less noise but obviously a fair amount of buffeting. The hood was made from pvc material, divided into three sections. Erection and dismantling was quick and easy, with a neat and sensible method of stowing away the hood irons behind the seats.

In the cockpit, some drivers felt a little too close to the wheel, but in general the controls were all well placed. Through the wheel, the driver could read the speedometer and the rev-counter, with supplementary, fuel, oil pressure and water temperature gauges.

Luggage accommodation was unusually arranged, the compartment was reached after folding down the seats (there was no boot 'lid'). Stowage and removal of the spare wheel were not therefore ideal, but again this simple design kept costs down. With the use of soft bags, a greater total volume of luggage could be carried than in many similar sized sports cars.

The mounting of the headlamps above the bonnet line was dictated by the minimum height regulations in the USA. Although 'imposed' on the design of the Sprite, it soon became the car's trade mark.

For access to the engine, the whole bonnet assembly, complete with lamps swung up on two supports. The lock and safety catch were not easy to reach and lifting the heavy assembly was not easy. The fact that the whole front could thus be removed has allowed for many Frogeye

GENERAL SPECIFICATION

Engine
Head/block	cast iron
Cylinders	4 in line
Bore/stroke	62·9 × 76·2 mm
Capacity	948 cc
Cooling	water
Valve gear	overhead pushrod
Compression	8·3:1
Carburettor	twin SU H1
Max. power	45 bhp at 5,500 rpm
Max. torque	52 lb-ft at 3,000 rpm

Transmission
Type	4-speed manual
Gear ratios	
Top	1·000:1
3rd	1·412:1
2nd	2·374:1
1st	3·627:1
Final drive	4·220:1

Suspension
Front	independent by coil springs, wishbones
Rear	quarter-elliptic springs, anti-roll bar

Steering
Type	BMC rack and pinion
Assistance	no

Brakes
Front	Lockheed 7-in drum
Rear	Lockheed 7-in drum
Servo	no

Wheels
Type	pressed steel
Tyres	5·20–13 in

Electrical
Battery	12v, 43 a-h
Earth	positive
Dynamo	Lucas
Headlamps	42/36W

The cockpit reflected the car's low cost

models to be renovated and made to look like new with glassfibre fronts, or for the purists, new aluminium bonnets.

The Sprite only had a small 6 gallon tank, but thanks to the car's economical nature this still allowed for a cruising range in excess of 200 miles.

The Austin-Healey Sprite had a charm that has grown with many motoring enthusiasts and it began a long line of small British sports cars. The Mk II Sprite appeared in the Spring of 1961 with a completely new body. Gone were the 'frogeyes' to be replaced with a smart, but somehow undistinguished new body shape. A year later the car received the 1,098 cc version of the A-Series engine to boost the power to 55 bhp and the top speed to 90 mph. It was also by then available with another name, as a badge-engineered MG Midget. The Sprite Mk III (Midget Mk II) came in 1964, now with disc brakes and semi-elliptic rear suspension. 1966 saw the Mk IV Sprite (Mk III Midget) with the Cooper S 1,275 cc engine.

Austin-Healey production was phased out in 1971 when a total of 129,354 had been built. The MG Midget variant continued and received the Triumph 1,500 cc engine in 1974. It also received the same squashy bumpers and raised suspension indignities that befell the MGB. No longer such a cheap sports car, the MG Midget soldiered on, desperately in need of further development to produce a 'new' Midget until production finally ceased at the end of 1979.

PERFORMANCE DATA
Date of test 20th June 1958

Maximum speeds	*mph*
Top	80
3rd	63
2nd	37
1st	23

Acceleration from rest	
mph	*sec*
0–30	5·3
0–50	13·7
0–60	20·9
0–70	35·6

Standing ¼ mile	21·7

Acceleration in	top	3rd
mph	*sec*	*sec*
10–30	—	8·6
20–40	12·7	8·3
30–50	12·3	9·2
40–60	17·2	12·7

Fuel consumption
Overall 34 mpg
Tank capacity 6 gal.
Max. range 204 miles

AC Ace

Britain's first independently sprung sports car was unveiled by AC at the 1953 London Motor Show, and the Ace was as attractive as it was advanced. Its looks were inspired by the Touring-bodied Barchetta 166 Ferrari, and under the skin designer John Tojeiro followed his usual practice of having a ladder-type chassis and independent suspension by lower wishbones and transverse leaf springs front and rear. This stiff frame led to roadholding and handling that was nothing short of sensational in 1953.

The power plant for the Ace was not so new. The first models had the famous AC 1,991 cc six-cylinder ohc engine designed by John Weller in 1919, producing 85 bhp at 4,500 rpm, and this remained available in the Ace as an option until 1963. However, the high qualities of the rest of the car led to a demand for more performance, and the ohv 1,971 cc straight six Bristol engine was therefore fitted to the Ace in 1956; this unit gave 120 bhp at 6,000 rpm.

When we tested an AC Ace-Bristol in 1958 it was unrivalled in the 2-litre sports car class. The ability to approach 120 mph and cover a quarter-mile from a standing start in $16\frac{1}{2}$ seconds was altogether exceptional for a production sports car with full touring equipment. Three Solex carburettors were matched to the Bristol engine, ensuring that power delivery was strong and unhesitant throughout the speed range.

The manual choke always brought about a sure start. It was wise, with an engine so tuned, to allow the engine a few minutes to warm before moving off from cold. A pull-out knob of the facia enabled the driver to retard the ignition when the engine was idling, and this increased tractability at low engine speeds when driving in traffic. With this control operating, the Bristol engine pulled smoothly and evenly at 20 mph in top gear – about 1,000 rpm.

Really useful torque delivery began at about 2,500 rpm, and there were no gaps in the power curve up to the recommended

All the instruments were grouped in front of the driver. The steering wheel shown is not original

rev limit of 6,000 rpm. The engine felt at its liveliest at around 4,500 rpm (about 90 mph in top) which gave the Ace the upper hand over practically anything it was likely to meet on the road up to about 110 mph. Thereafter it climbed a little more slowly to its 116–118 mph maximum speed.

Mean acceleration figures quoted in the acceleration panel tell much of the story of the Ace's progress; standstill to 30 mph in 3·5 sec, to 60 mph in 9·1 sec, and 90 mph in 19·9 sec. At any engine speed above 2,500 rpm the response to a decision to overtake was immediate. Although the engine was reasonably quiet mechanically, full-throttle driving produced a rather invigorating commotion under the bonnet. The exhaust note was at its loudest at 4,000 rpm, but was never excessive or objectionable and in town the Ace could be motored as quietly as necessary.

The Bristol engine was fitted with a gearbox of the same make, with synchromesh on all except first speed. Ideally matched, the ratios allowed maxima exceeding 40, 60 or 90 mph in the three indirect gears. The gear lever had a short and precise movement. The gearbox was commendably quiet and the final drive inaudible.

Fuel consumption with a car of this performance potential, which was designed to be driven hard, was not a strong selling point, but around 22–25 mpg was the likely average. With a standard fuel capacity of 13 gallons, the safe touring range was thus about 250 miles.

On reasonable road surfaces the AC driver had little to complain about. Once the car was moving fast the firmness of the suspension paid valuable dividends in exceptional stability. Moreover, at the car's cruising speeds – 90 mph and more was commonplace – the ride was comfortable and level.

When there was any loss of adhesion on a

bend, it occurred first at the rear end, and the driver received some initial warning of it. There was negligible roll and little pitch, although over poor surfaces there was a noticeable up and down movement at the front of the car.

The steering was quite high geared, but light in normal use and agreeably precise at all times. At fast speeds, the directional stability of the AC was excellent, with only finger-tip steering necessary. Within the limitations of normal road use the Ace had no handling 'tricks' – and success in competition confirmed that it was equally manageable at racing speeds.

Disc brakes were an option at the front, and were fitted to the test car. No servo assistance was provided, but a fairly long pedal movement allowed for sufficient leverage, the pedal pressures necessary for even a rapid stop being moderate and in normal conditions the brakes were extremely smooth and even.

Exterior door handles were not provided, the hinged section of the side windows had to be opened to reach the interior handles. Even if exterior handles had been fitted the car could not be locked because the detachable hood had exposed fasteners. The hood itself was particularly neat and reasonably draught-free, although at speed the hood could lift sufficiently to open a gap between it and the tops of the sidescreens.

The bucket seats needed a little more rake in the backrests, the cushions themselves being comfortable (they were trimmed in leather, as was the facia and glove box). The main instruments were placed quite low on the facia and were a little difficult to read, being partially masked by the steering wheel spokes.

A wide transmission tunnel divided the floor area, with two small vertical tubes passing through this to add support to the scuttle. It was a great credit to the Ace's chassis that scuttle shake was completely absent – quite an achievement in a car with such a simple frame.

The AC Ace-Bristol offerd a rewarding

Clean lines require no adornment. Wire wheels were standard

GENERAL SPECIFICATION

Engine
Head/block	cast iron/alloy
Cylinders	6 in line
Bore/stroke	66 × 96 mm
Capacity	1,971 cc
Cooling	water
Valve gear	overhead pushrod
Compression	9:1
Carburettor	3 Solex 32PBI6
Max. power	120 bhp at 6,000 rpm
Max. torque	123 lb-ft at 3,750 rpm

Transmission
Type	4-speed manual
Gear ratios	
Top	1·000:1
3rd	1·402:1
2nd	1·798:1
1st	2·921:1
Final drive	3·910:1

Suspension
Front	independent by single transverse leaf and lower wishbone
Rear	independent by single transverse leaf and lower wishbone

Steering
Type	Bishop cam and lever
Assistance	no

Brakes
Front	Girling 11·75-in disc
Rear	Girling 11-in drum
Servo	no

Wheels
Type	centre-lock wire
Tyres	5·50–16 in

Electrical
Battery	12v, 60 a-h
Earth	positive
Dynamo	Lucas
Headlamps	48/36W

The Ace's neat engine installation. The straight-six power plant had three Solex carburettors

PERFORMANCE DATA
Date of test 7th November 1958

Maximum speeds		mph
Top		117
3rd		94
2nd		66
1st		41

Acceleration from rest	
mph	sec
0–30	3·5
0–40	4·7
0–50	6·8
0–60	9·1
0–70	12·4
0–80	15·8
0–90	19·9
0–100	27·0
0–110	40·4

Standing ¼ mile 16·5

Acceleration in	top	3rd
mph	sec	sec
20–40	—	6·7
30–50	8·9	6·4
40–60	8·7	5·9
50–70	8·5	6·0
60–80	8·6	6·5
70–90	10·0	7·3
80–100	12·6	—
90–110	19·7	—

Fuel consumption
Overall   22 mpg
Tank capacity 13 gal.
Max. range   286 miles

combination of speed, acceleration, with very safe handling, and good brakes and steering. In 1954 the Aceca coupe had been added to the AC range with its curved rear screen and, later to be so popular, a hinged rear window panel. The Bristol engine was also available in this variant from 1956. In 1960 the longer wheelbase four-seater Greyhound was introduced with the Bristol engine. When supplies of this power plant threatened to dry up the Ford Zephyr engine was offered for the Ace and Aceca.

By far the most famous development of the AC Ace was, of course, the AC Cobra. American Carroll Shelby recognized the potential of the Ace's chassis and suggested it should take the compact short stroke Ford V8 engine. With suitable strengthening to the chassis and suspension, AC production of this Anglo-American hybrid began in 1963. Cobras built up a splendid racing record, with the Daytona coupe version winning the 1965 world GT championship. The Cobra's engine increased in size first to the 4·7-litre V8 producing 271 bhp in standard form and then came what is probably the ultimate 'muscle' car. The addition of fatter tyres and wider wheel arches distinguished the AC Cobra 427, with a 7-litre V8 engine from the Ford Galaxy, a 345 bhp and 160 mph sports car!

When Cobra production ceased in 1968, 1,019 had been built, and those that remain are cherished classics.

Austin-Healey 3000

The 1952 London Motor Show saw the debut of Donald Healey's graceful open two-seater called simply the '100'. It had the 2·6-litre four-cylinder engine from the Austin A90 and various other proprietary Austin parts in a simple ladder-type chassis, with wishbone coil sprung independent front suspension and a rigid axle on leaf springs at the rear. The engine was just capable of powering the car to 102 mph, thus justifying the name.

Austin were at the time thinking of producing a stock-based sports car and the good looks of the 100 soon led to an agreement that allowed Austin to use the Healey name, and production of the Austin-Healey 100 began at Longbridge in 1953.

The car fitted nicely into the market place, in the gap between Triumph or MG and Jaguar, with especially high demand coming from America. Modified versions appeared later with the 100-Six coming in 1956 (this had the BMC 2·6-litre six-cylinder engine giving 102 bhp, and a longer, restyled body). The success of these models meant that development followed and progressed to the first Austin-Healey 3000 which appeared in 1959.

In general appearance the larger Austin-Healey had changed little since its 1952 debut. The major differences for 1959 was the 2,912 cc 124 bhp engine, a strengthened chassis and 11-in disc brakes at the front.

Improved acceleration, particularly above 70 mph and appreciable increases in maximum speed resulted from the larger engine. Compared with our road test of the 100-Six, which was fitted with a 4·1 to 1 axle ratio compared to the 3000's 3·9 to 1 there was a cut of 4·9 seconds off the 0–100 mph time. In overdrive top there was an increase of 5 mph, to give a top speed of 116 mph. These figures were a good indication that the 2·9 litre engine was well able to deal with the extra weight and higher final drive gearing of this latest Austin-Healey.

None of the low-speed characteristics of the previous model were lost, however, the car pulling well at low throttle and being

easy and comfortable to drive in traffic. Well mannered as the car was in towns, it made the driver impatient to get to the open roads where the full performance could be savoured. Cruising at 100 mph was possible without any evidence of mechanical distress.

One of the optional extras fitted to the test car was a Laycock-de Normanville overdrive operating on third and top gears. This worked well, not only in keeping the engine speed down, and thus aiding fuel economy, but also keeping the noise lower so as not to tire the occupants on a long journey. The overdrive control switch was on the right of the facia, with changes into and out of overdrive being snatch-free and immediate.

The gear ratios were well-suited to the performance of the engine and the car. Third and top were pleasantly close, with acceleration in second and third being in the 'kick-in-the-back variety' – care was necessary on wet roads to avoid wheelspin with full throttle.

Little difference was made to the steering and suspension of the car by the extra weight compared to that of the previous model (the greater percentage of the extra weight was still over the rear axle). When tested we concluded that the car handled well, with the rear having a tendency to swing when cornering on slippery roads. The suspension was well-damped, and firm enough to ensure that the car did not roll when cornering fast. It was also noted that ground clearance was low (a fact that made the car's rallying successes all the more impressive).

The front disc, rear drum, brake set-up at all times proved excellent, although pedal pressures were a little high for normal check-braking as no servo was fitted.

Driver comfort was marred by the lack of room around the pedals, while the seats were a little 'thin' and lacked lateral support, making them rather uncomfortable after a long drive.

The test car was fitted with the optional hardtop, and although thought to be a little expensive – it cost £85 in 1959 – it was considered a desirable extra. Light in weight, it was easily removed. Some even

The Mk II version had three SU carburettors, and developed 132 bhp

The small child seat in the rear could be folded for increased luggage space

Top: The smart two-tone paintwork gave the car a purposeful look. Note the limited ground clearance

Above: The optional hard-top was thought a desirable extra

felt it improved the car's look. The standard conventional folding hood offered satisfactory protection at the expense of increased noise when driving fast.

Visibility was good, the screen pillars commendably thin, the top of each wing could be seen, with headroom satisfactory for even a tall driver. It was not really practical for an adult to try and sit on the rear 'bench' of the car with the hood-up, as even a child was restricted severely by lack of head or leg room.

The interior layout had changed little from the 100 with the instruments grouped in pairs on either side of the steering

GENERAL SPECIFICATION

Engine
Head/block	cast iron
Cylinders	6 in line
Bore/stroke	83·36 × 88·90 mm
Capacity	2,912 cc
Cooling	water
Valve gear	overhead pushrod
Compression	9:1
Carburettor	2 SU HD6
Max. power	124 bhp at 4,600 rpm
Max. torque	175 lb-ft at 3,000 rpm

Transmission
Type	4-speed manual, plus overdrive
Gear ratios	
Overdrive	0·820:1
Top	1·000:1
3rd	1·309:1
2nd	2·053:1
1st	2·930:1
Final drive	3·909:1

Suspension
Front	independent by coil springs, wishbones, anti-roll bar
Rear	half-elliptic leaf springs, Panhard rod

Steering
Type	Cam Gears cam and peg
Assistance	no

Brakes
Front	Girling 11¼-in disc
Rear	Girling 11-in drum
Servo	no

Wheels
Type	centre-lock wire
Tyres	5·90–15 in

Electrical
Battery	12v, 57 a-h
Earth	positive
Dynamo	Lucas C45PV6
Headlamps	50/40W

The interior changed little from the original 100-Six

column. Luggage accommodation was severely limited, as the spare wheel and the battery took up a large proportion of the space in the boot. A battery master switch was a useful security device as it was not possible to lock the boot of this first model.

The immediate conclusion was that this Austin-Healey maintained the reputation of the marque as a good quality, fast sports-touring car – this was very apt as the 'big Healeys' grew in popularity, a popularity that remains to this day and has established them as a true classic.

Development progressed, with the Mk II 3000 appearing in 1961 with a triple-carburettor engine developing 132 bhp, in the following year, the engine reverted to twin carburettors with the Mk III 3000 announced in 1964. This final version had 148 bhp on tap and a top speed of 123 mph as well as rather more 'civilized' equipment such as wind-up windows. There was even a Mk IV project featuring a 4-litre engine, but in the face of forthcoming American safety regulations this was scrapped and Austin-Healey 3000 production ceased with 43,000 having been produced.

The rally successes of the big Healeys achieved almost legendary status with the most famous probably being the red 3000 driven by Pat Moss. The Austin-Healey 3000 achieved no less than 40 outright class victories in major events, despite that lack of ground clearance. . . .

PERFORMANCE DATA
Date of test 28th August 1959

Maximum speeds	mph	
Overdrive	116	
Top	110	
3rd	78	
2nd	49	
1st	34	

Acceleration from rest		
mph	sec	
0–30	3·5	
0–40	5·6	
0–50	8·0	
0–60	11·4	
0–70	14·3	
0–80	18·9	
0–90	24·8	
0–100	32·8	

Standing ¼ mile 17·9

Acceleration in	top	3rd
mph	sec	sec
20–40	9·0	6·8
30–50	9·0	6·8
40–60	9·0	7·1
50–70	9·5	7·3
60–80	10·3	8·4
70–90	13·0	10·4
80–100	16·7	13·9

Fuel consumption
Overall 20 mpg
Tank capacity 12 gal.
Max. range 240 miles

Daimler SP250

So different was the SP250 from what people expected from Daimler, that it was truly regarded as a complete breakaway from tradition. First seen at the New York Motor Show in 1959, where it was called the Dart, this sports car, from a previously rather sedate company, took the motoring world by surprise.

The SP250's engine was outstanding, the car's looks not quite so. The 2·5-litre V8 engine had a very short stroke, a five bearing crankshaft and a single camshaft operating inclined valves in hemispherical combustion chambers through pushrods, producing a claimed 140 bhp. This compact light alloy engine was fitted to a short cross-braced chassis with underslung half-elliptic springs at the rear enclosed in what can best be described as a 'controversial' glassfibre body.

First impressions of the SP250 ('Dart' had to be dropped due to prior use of the name) that we had to test was that it had the layout and equipment expected of a sports car with several 'luxury' features typical of a company like Daimler. The facia for example was padded with a leather overlay, the interior trimmed in leather-bound carpeting, and the seats were also leather upholstered. The 'occasional' rear bench was of no use for an adult when the front seats were positioned for taller drivers as there was then no leg room at all. It was, however, suitable for children, or for additional luggage space.

From the driver's seat, visibility was good with slim screen pillars, while the sloping nose with separate side lamps and the rear wing tips were excellent aids for the driver to judge manoeuvres. Pedal pressures were light, the throttle being smooth and progressive.

Glassfibre bodies, though not strictly new, were still something of a novelty in 1959. It was reported right from the outset that the SP250 required greater rigidity and attention to detail finish. This fact was further underlined as more SP250s got

A most striking, and controversial, design

onto the roads and drivers reported that the whole car flexed to an alarming degree, and that the doors flew open during cornering. By 1961, the chassis had been strengthened and the bodywork itself made to a much better specification, helping to relieve the problem.

The V8 engine was always an instant starter, hot or cold. It had a pleasing, deep, twin exhaust note which over about 4,000 rpm developed into a 'bark' that was thought at the time to be rather too loud for most British tastes. Very flexible, the engine would pull strongly from as little as 1,000 rpm in top gear, at no time was it fussy, or mechanically noisy.

Considering the size of the engine and the performance available, fuel consumption was extremely light. After nearly 1,500 miles of testing we recorded an overall consumption figure of 29·1 mpg. Oil consumption was rather high – during the test the SP250 consumed no less than two gallons!

Performance testing showed the car to have a top speed of 121 mph, a standing quarter mile of 18 sec and a 0 to 100 mph figure of 26·3 sec. These impressive acceleration figures were taken on a car that seemed to have a fraction of clutch slip. In spite of a live axle and rear suspension that was rather conventional for the period, there was no axle hop during fierce getaways, which was much to the car's credit.

The gear ratios were thought to be about right for the car and engine. Gear changes, however, were not up to the same high standard, and it was difficult to avoid a growl or grunt when making rapid changes up through the gears. Leisurely changes were satisfactory, but with faster changes it was possible to beat the synchromesh.

Probably the car's best feature, the excellent V8 engine

The glassfibre body was something of a novelty for 1959

Up to the Daimler standard, the instrument panel had a padded leather overlay

Second and third gears were particularly rewarding when driving fast, with 72 mph available in second, and 106 mph in third. Automatic transmission or a Laycock overdrive could be specified as an option.

On a car with such performance, the brakes obviously needed to be of a high standard. Girling discs were fitted to all four wheels; smooth and powerful, they did their job well.

The ride was firm and lively, without being harsh – very typical in fact of a live axle sports car. The rear wheels were prone to patter a little on uneven surfaces and, as already mentioned, considerable body flexing – with the passenger's door opening on two occasions during our test. The steering was rather heavy and dead in feel. The rear end could be forced to break away, but this was easily caught and corrected.

GENERAL SPECIFICATION

Engine
Head/block	alloy/cast iron
Cylinders	8 in 90° vee
Bore/stroke	76·20 × 69·85 mm
Capacity	2,548 cc
Cooling	water
Valve gear	overhead pushrod
Compression	8·2:1
Carburettor	twin SU HD6
Max. power	140 bhp at 5,800 rpm
Max. torque	155 lb-ft at 3,600 rpm

Transmission
Type	4-speed manual
Gear Ratios	
Top	1·000:1
3rd	1·232:1
2nd	1·743:1
1st	2·933:1
Final drive	3·580:1

Suspension
Front	independent by coil springs, wishbones
Rear	live axle, half-elliptic leaf springs

Steering
Type	Cam Gears cam and lever
Assistance	no

Brakes
Front	Girling 10·62–in disc
Rear	Girling 10-in disc
Servo	no

Wheels
Type	pressed steel
Tyres	5·90–15 in

Electrical
Battery	12v, 57 a-h
Earth	positive
Dynamo	Lucas C40
Headlamps	45/40W

The interior was well finished and fully carpeted

PERFORMANCE DATA		
Date of test 2nd October 1959		
Maximum speeds	*mph*	
Top	121	
3rd	106	
2nd	72	
1st	44	
Acceleration from rest		
mph	*sec*	
0–30	3·8	
0–40	5·4	
0–50	7·7	
0–60	10·2	
0–70	12·9	
0–80	17·5	
0–90	21·8	
0–100	26·3	
0–110	35·6	
Standing ¼ mile	17·8	
Acceleration	top	3rd
mph	*sec*	*sec*
10–30	8·9	7·2
20–40	8·7	6·3
30–50	8·1	6·2
40–60	7·9	6·1
50–70	7·8	5·7
60–80	8·1	6·2
70–90	8·5	7·6
80–100	10·9	9·5
Fuel consumption		
Overall	29·1 mpg	
Tank capacity	12 gal.	
Max. range	348 miles	

Although the SP250 was small and compact, it had a large boot capable of carrying far more luggage than most of its sports car competitors. The spare wheel was housed under the boot floor, which allowed for the extra space. There was also space to work on the engine, with all items necessary for inspection easily accessible.

Weather protection on the car was satisfactory, with a hood frame and material substantial enough to prevent flapping when erect. The only major point of criticism was the sealing flaps around the windows which did not fit very well.

The fuel tank had a capacity of 12 gallons, which coupled with the car's excellent fuel consumption, meant a touring range of some 350 miles between fill-ups. With the car's good luggage space, this made the SP250 a fine long distance tourer.

The SP250 promised a lot, and many thought it could be the first in a long line of Daimler sports cars. The car had many supporters – a number were even used by British police forces – but when Jaguar took control of Daimler in 1960 it was not the sort of car Sir William Lyons wanted to make, and despite the fact that it was no real competitor for the E-type, it was dropped in 1964. The engine survived a little longer, however, and was fitted into the Daimler 2·5-litre V8 saloon, which was based on the Mark 2 Jaguar; this model was a success and remained in production until the end of 1969.

Aston Martin DB4

Competition in the Grand Touring class of the 1950s was fierce, contenders from Britain such as AC, Alvis, Bristol and Jaguar competing with Continental marques like Ferrari, Maserati and Alfa Romeo. Undoubtedly, the British GT champion of the time was Aston Martin, and the car that led the way for them was the star of the 1958 London Motor Show, the Aston Martin DB4.

The DB4 had a direct development of the six-cylinder 3·7-litre alloy engine that had made its debut in the DBR sports racing car at the 1957 Le Mans 24 Hour Race, and its platform-type chassis carried a shapely aluminium body styled by Superleggera Touring of Italy.

With its race-proved coil spring and wishbone front suspension, but with a live axle and coil springs at the rear, the DB4 had the performance and the road manners – coupled with the high quality finish – to justify the maker's claim that the car was '. . . the ultimate symbol of success'.

From its introduction to our 1961 road test, the DB4 received a number of significant modifications. Laycock de Normanville overdrive was made available, and a new type of Borg and Beck two-plate clutch was fitted, there was the option of a 3·31-to-1 final drive ratio, without overdrive of course, the original 4·09-to-1 ratio having been dropped. In addition the ratios of second and third gears were lowered numerically by 12 per cent, and a modified radiator grille replaced the original pattern with narrow, closely spaced horizontal slats.

In the car, the detail, functional layout and finish were impressive. Everything except the chrome instrument bezel was black and non-reflecting; the leather of the upholstery, scuttle, facia and the padded roll along its top edge and the matt finish of the instrument surround, even the spokes of the lightweight, alloy and laminated wood steering wheel were, in the true fashion of the time, finished in matt black.

The full quota of dials grouped directly in front of the driver in a hooded panel were clearly visible when the road wheels were in the straight ahead position. Markings on

The DB4's aluminium body was styled by Superleggera Touring of Italy

The beautifully finished engine completely filled the underbonnet space

The driver had a full quota of instruments directly ahead

the speedometer and rev-counter were large, easily taken in at a glance – the whole layout reflected the years of competition work behind the car. The whole compartment was divided fore and aft by the high hump covering the clutch and gearbox, and the short gear lever was placed precisely where the driver's left hand dropped on it.

The view through the wide sloping screen was excellent, with sensibly thin screen pillars. The seats had a wide range of fore and aft and rake adjustment, so that it was possible to tailor the position to suit drivers of all shapes and sizes. The driver sat very high, though with adequate head clearance, very much in command of the

car. The DB4 was claimed to be a four-seater, but the shape of the body would not really allow four adults to remain in comfort for long journeys (the rear compartment was, however, fully and comfortably upholstered).

The engine started from cold immediately and soon warmed to working temperature. Its tractability in traffic was impressive – despite being able to top 140 mph, the DB4 would trickle along in top gear at just 15 mph and would accelerate very smoothly from this speed when the throttle was floored, making the car very docile in traffic.

For the car's 240 bhp to be used to the full, liberal use of the gearbox was necessary. The ratios were very well-spaced – second and third took the car to 76 and 115 mph respectively at the recommended limit of 5,800 rpm. In normal main road traffic moving at around 60 mph, every possible opportunity to overtake could be used.

The clutch pedal travel was rather too long for comfort, and due to the increased drag of the two-plate clutch, the pedal had to be depressed fully to the floor before first could be engaged at rest; pedal pressure too was high and tended to become tiresome in traffic. In performance, however, it was smooth and progressive.

Steering was quick and positive, directional stability being arrow-like, the car maintaining a dead-straight line right up to the car's maximum. Some road shocks were transmitted to the wheel, although this had little effect on the car's stability.

By the sports car standards of the time the suspension was soft and well able to absorb long-frequency undulations on main roads, providing a steady and comfortable ride. Despite the relative softness of the suspension, any incitement to pitch was damped out effectively. There was little roll, however fast the car was cornered. There were no vices or idiosyncrasies in the handling, and one quickly acquired a sense of confidence in the car. In the wet the rear wheels could be induced to slide outwards, but correction was quick and easy.

On a car of this sort good brakes are obviously of vital importance. The DB4's hydraulic servo-assisted Dunlop discs were thought at the time to be probably the best we had tested. The only criticism was that

GENERAL SPECIFICATION	
Engine	
Head/block	alloy
Cylinder	6 in line
Bore/stroke	92 × 92 mm
Capacity	3,670 cc
Cooling	water
Valve gear	twin ohc
Compression	8·25:1
Carburettor	twin SU HD8
Max. power	240 bhp at 5,500 rpm
Max. torque	240 lb-ft at 4,250 rpm
Transmission	
Type	4-speed manual
Gear ratios	
Top	1·000:1
3rd	1·251:1
2nd	1·855:1
1st	2·921:1
Final drive	3·54:1
Suspension	
Front	transverse wishbones, co-axial coil springs
Rear	live axle, coil springs, parallel trailing links, transverse Watts linkage
Steering	
Type	rack and pinion
Assistance	no
Brakes	
Front	Dunlop 12·12-in disc
Rear	Dunlop 11·12-in disc
Wheels	
Type	centre-lock wire
Tyres	6·00–16 in
Electrical	
Battery	12v, 51 a-h
Earth	positive
Dynamo	Lucas
Headlamps	45/40W

This modified grille replaced the original horizontally slatted one

The stylish back end of the Aston Martin had a steeply raked rear window

PERFORMANCE DATA
Date of test 13th October 1961

Maximum speeds	mph
Top	140
3rd	115
2nd	76
1st	46

Acceleration from rest	
mph	sec
0–30	3·5
0–40	4·9
0–50	6·7
0–60	8·5
0–70	10·6
0–80	12·5
0–90	17·7
0–100	21·7
0–110	26·0
0–120	34·6
0–130	44·8

Standing ¼ mile	16·1

Acceleration in	top	3rd
mph	sec	sec
10–30	—	6·9
20–40	8·2	6·4
30–50	8·2	6·2
40–60	8·9	6·4
50–70	8·7	6·5
60–80	9·0	6·6
70–90	9·1	6·6
80–100	10·5	7·2
90–110	11·1	7·9
100–120	13·7	—
110–130	17·4	—

Fuel consumption	
Overall	16·4 mpg
Tank capacity	19 gal.
Max. range	310 miles

as the pads were hard they were a little lacking in 'bite' until fully warmed.

The boot was fully carpeted, free from obstruction, and ample for two peoples' luggage. The battery was behind a panel on the right, with the tool kit behind a similar panel on the left – and as with all Aston Martins since, the tool kit was both comprehensive and of the highest quality.

Under-bonnet accessibility was excellent, the radiator header tank and filler cap mounted to the left, with the oil level dipstick extending right up to the level of the cam-covers. A remarkably comprehensive instruction book, leather bound – in keeping with the rest of the car – told the owner all he needed to know.

The DB4 was a touring car in the grand manner, a car in which great distances could be covered in short times. It was reasonably quiet, with performance and controllability of such a high order it was a pleasure to drive.

A very significant model in the Aston Martin history, the DB4 was the last car to be built at Feltham before the company moved to their present location in Newport Pagnell in 1964. In that same year the DB4 engine was given a slightly larger bore, increasing the capacity to 3,995 cc, coupled to a five-speed gearbox, the car became the DB5. A slightly longer wheelbase version, the DB6, was introduced two years later with even more 'GT' refinements; electric windows, power steering and the option of automatic transmission. The lengthened roofline of the DB6 made the car a roomier two-door four-seater, but in looks it did not quite match up to the elegance of line of the original DB4.

Sunbeam Tiger 260

The Sunbeam Alpine was announced by the Rootes Group in 1959. Despite its looks, it was never a full-blooded sports car, really more of an open tourer with sporting characteristics. Even with the addition of the 92·5 bhp 1,725 cc engine for the Series V Alpine, in 1965, it could not reach the magic 100 mph.

Attempts to use the Alpine in competition were also thwarted, and the impetus to make the car become a *real* sports car came from the USA. The success of the AC Cobra (a big American engine in a well-prepared AC Ace chassis, see page 38) led a Sunbeam dealer in the West Coast of America to ask the Cobra's originator, Carroll Shelby, to install a 4·2-litre Ford V8 into a Series IV Alpine. This prototype was tested by Rootes and then actually put into production in 1965.

The idea of 'mill switching' was therefore, not new. What was unprecedented at the time, however, was for a large British manufacturer to install a foreign engine from a rival firm. What also surprised was the fact that the changed car felt so balanced – a great credit to the basic Alpine design, the characteristics of the engine and the development of the installation.

The V8 Fairlane engine fitted had a Borg-Warner four-speed gearbox, with the final drive gearing raised from 3·89 to 2·88 to 1, giving 23·9 mph per 1,000 rpm. Other engineering changes necessary for the Alpine were a cross-flow radiator with a larger matrix area and a remote header tank, rack and pinion steering (the Alpine had recirculating ball), and the new position of the battery, in the boot.

The engine produced 164 bhp gross. Much more significant, however, was the peak torque figure of 258 lb-ft. The penalty for this increased power was increased weight, up some 448 lb on the Alpine. The benefit in performance was significant, with the Tiger's time to 80 mph of 17·5 sec being almost *half* that of the Alpine, and the maximum speed of 117 mph being 20 mph faster.

If required, the Tiger would remain as

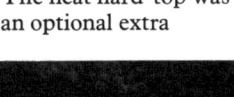
The neat hard-top was an optional extra

This car has a non-standard, and more modern, steering wheel

sweet and docile as other contemporary family cars. The non-sporting characteristics (and origins) of the engine were felt when accelerating, for although the rev-counter was red-lined at 4,700 rpm, the car's pull fell off progressively from 1,000 rpm below that, and one never really needed to even approach the limit. After learning to change up early when accelerating and not to bother with changing down unless the speed had really dropped, the Tiger was a rapid and enjoyable car to drive.

Narrow though the rev band might have been, the speed ranges in the gears were unusually wide. First had a maximum of 54 mph, when required, and top would pull from as low as 10 mph.

In the wet, rather more delicate control was needed to avoid axle tramp which, if allowed to continue, would have damaged the rear suspension. Once the clutch was fully home, however, full throttle could be used in either first or second without any trace of snaking or rear-end twitchiness, provided the car was pointing straight. Cornering on slippery surfaces called for caution, although within a very short time it was possible to learn how far the tail would kick out and thus anticipate the required steering correction. Power drifting, even in the dry, was particularly easy in the Tiger. One ran into the corners on the overrun to a point just short of the apex, then unwound the lock and stamped on the throttle at the same time. The tail would slide out just so far and then stop on its own as the weight transferred back under power and added to the rear end grip. Normally when driving round beds at a steady speed the handling had just a trace of understeer with a strong self-centring action. This gave good stability at speed, with a good deal of feed back to the steering wheel of any road irregularities.

In ride comfort the Tiger felt much like the Alpine. There was a good balance between firm control of the wheels for tidy handling and soft movements to avoid shocks. Certain types of surfaces could catch the backend by surprise, especially in a corner when the tail could patter sideways a foot or so.

Starting the engine from cold was always simple and immediate, once the throttle had been blipped to catch the automatic choke. No warming-up period was necessary before the engine would pull strongly and without hesitation.

Fuel consumption was in the region of 17–20 mpg, which meant that with the twin 5½ gallon tanks, maximum range between fill-ups was about 220 miles.

At around 80 mph there was considerable wind roar with the (optional) hard top in place. With the standard hood erected there was much more noise generally, but no flapping. In open trim buffeting was not too unpleasant. Motoring in any of these three forms emphasized the near-absence of mechanical noise from the engine. The folded pvc hood was well-hidden behind the tonneau cover, and was simple to erect, giving snug and weather-tight protection, although the blind rear three-quarters did cut down visibility at times.

The Tiger's brakes were identical to those of the Alpine, discs at the front with servo assistance, and coped extremely well with the extra performance.

To accommodate the larger engine, a few inches of leg room were sacrificed, but this was hardly obvious once in the car. The

Below: twin spotlights were fitted to the Tiger

Bottom: the rear 'fins' were typical of the period

GENERAL SPECIFICATION

Engine
Head/block	cast iron
Cylinders	8 in 90° vee
Bore/stroke	96·5 ×73 mm
Capacity	4,261 cc
Cooling	water
Valve gear	overhead pushrod
Compression	8·8:1
Carburettor	Ford twin-choke
Max. power	164 bhp at 4,400 rpm
Max. torque	258 lb-ft at 2,200 rpm

Transmission
Type	4-speed manual
Gear ratios	
Top	1·00:1
3rd	1·29:1
2nd	1·69:1
1st	2·32:1
Final drive	2·88:1

Suspension
Front	independent by coil springs, wishbones, anti-roll bar
Rear	live axle, half-elliptic leaf springs, Panhard rod

Steering
Type	rack and pinion
Assistance	no

Brakes
Front	Girling 9·85-in disc
Rear	Girling 9-in drum
Servo	yes

Wheels
Type	pressed-steel disc
Tyres	5·90–13 in

Electrical
Battery	12v, 67 a-h
Earth	negative
Dynamo	Ford C40F (360W)

Seemingly shoe-horned under the bonnet, 4,261 cc of Ford V8 Fairlane engine

Following pages: This particular bright red Tiger has non-standard alloy wheels

only noticeable alteration was the fact that the pedal cluster was no longer movable, although the steering wheel was adjustable for reach. Most drivers were therefore able to get comfortable behind the wheel, the seats being adjustable for reach and rake.

In front of the driver there was a comprehensive set of instruments. The heater was fine for driving with the top down, a good deal of heat was available to the nether regions through the footwells. There was, however, no independent cold air ventilation, which meant with the hood up in the summer it could get a trifle stuffy with a considerable amount of engine and transmission heat transmitted to the cockpit.

When concluding the road test we were at pains to point out that the Tiger was somewhat misnamed, as there was nothing of the wild and dangerous about the car. If necessary the car could be very subdued, but the power was there, and available without fuss, noise or effort.

The Tiger was not to have a long life. Industrial problems in 1967 saw the Rootes company taken over by Chrysler. The new owners were naturally acutely embarassed about using a Ford engine, and as they did not have a suitable replacement for it, the Tiger was unceremoniously dropped that same year, with the Alpine following in 1968. Some 7,000 had been built at that time, including a few Tiger IIs which were fitted with the even more potent 4,727 cc Ford V8 engine.

PERFORMANCE DATA
Date of test 30th April 1965

Maximum speeds		*mph*
Top		117
3rd		98
2nd		74
1st		54

Acceleration from rest	
mph	*sec*
0–30	3·2
0–40	5·0
0–50	6·8
0–60	9·5
0–70	12·4
0–80	17·5
0–90	22·4
0–100	32·5
0–110	45·8

Standing ¼ mile	17·0

Acceleration in	top	3rd
mph	*sec*	*sec*
10–30	6·6	5·1
20–40	5·8	4·8
30–50	5·8	4·5
40–60	6·0	4·6
50–70	6·8	5·3
60–80	7·7	6·1
70–90	9·0	9·8
80–100	11·9	—
90–110	19·2	—

Fuel consumption
Overall 16·9 mpg
Tank capacity 11·25 gal.
Max. range 190 miles

MG MGB GT

The MGB was a logical replacement to the MGA when it was introduced in 1962. Its pressed-steel monocoque construction bodyshell, in place of the MGA's separate chassis frame, made it a thoroughly up-to-date sports car when it first appeared. Its sleek lines were much admired and coupled to the fact that it was faster than any previous MG it began to sell in large quantities.

In 1965 the MGB range was extended by the addition of the sports coupe version, the MGB GT. This complemented a trend for fixed-head sports cars and was an instant 'hit' for the 'Swinging Sixties' when it was unveiled at the 1965 London Motor Show.

By comparison to the open MGB it was thought a little costly. The 1966 price was £998 – without optional extras like a heater, wire wheels or radio – and this was some £143 more than its open stablemate. The extra cost, however, was accounted for by the much better finish of this volume produced sports coupe compared to some of its competitors, the more specialist, and much smaller, sports car manufacturers.

By adding a metal top, with all the extra glass and trim that entailed, as well as insulating the interior with heavy sound deadening materials, the overall weight of the coupe was increased by 200 lb. But the performance was only marginally inferior to the two-seater, and when comparing the steady fuel consumption of the two cars, the GT proved a little more economical.

Although the two models shared the same mechanical base, the difference in character between them was readily recognized as being between a sports and a sporting car. In the case of the coupe it was

thought particularly sensible to relate the road performance, in terms of figures, to the *manner* in which they are accomplished. Thus, although the 95 bhp for a 1·8-litre engine was a healthy figure for the time, the MGB GT could be out-accelerated by many touring saloons with engines no bigger. But none of these competitors could match the MG's tractability at low engine speeds, nor the cleanness in pick-up from 500 rpm in top gear. It was docile, free from temperament, and a car that was thought suitable for anyone (particularly women drivers, who appreciated a chic line but were not prepared to suffer the usual sports car traits). This 'character' made the car what it was.

The engine started easily, and warm-up was quick. It would run smoothly right through the rev range up to its limit of 6,000 rpm where it remained smooth and free from thrash or valve bounce but was noticeably more obtrusive to the ear.

In the lower gears, 6,000 rpm took the driver to 30 mph in first, 50 in second, 80 in third, and nearly 100 in overdrive third. There was a not inconsiderable jump in ratio from second to third, but the engine's full torque curve took care of this quite satisfactorily. The Laycock-de Normanville overdrive really cut the revs down and enabled high speeds to be maintained with little engine fuss, as well as reducing fuel consumption.

The gearbox had no synchromesh on first in these early models and was consequently very noisy in first and reverse, but except for some hiss from the constant mesh pinions was generally quiet. The clutch action was progressive and the pedal load moderate.

For our standing-start acceleration figures the road surface was damp but there was no apparent wheelspin. The MGB GT could be taken through fast corners with the tyres squealing, without any sudden breakaway. It had near enough neutral characteristics with a touch of initial understeer, and a fine fore-and-aft balance right up to the point where the tyres lost grip, when the rear tended to slide the most.

With just three turns lock-to-lock the steering was reasonably high geared and the rack-and-pinion provided reassuring precision with strong castor action and little feed back of shocks from the road wheels. Directional stability at speed was also thought to be very good.

The suspension was praised as having a high standard of roadholding expected of an MG without sacrificing ride comfort. A reasonably soft springing system, with good damper control avoided recurrent pitch without producing harshness.

Braking was balanced and progressive although there was criticism that one needed to push rather hard for a really quick stop and that a servo might be much appreciated.

The leather trimmed front seats were comfortable and resilient but rather in need of more lateral support in the backrests.

The distinctive front of an MGB

The coupe format gave added versatility to this sports car

Adjustable stops enabled the backrest angle to be altered a few degrees. Behind the seats there was a flat detachable bench cushion suitable for small children. This could be folded flat to increase the luggage load area. The luggage area was fully carpeted, with the plywood platform floor hinged for access to the spare wheel.

The pedals were offset to the right owing to the width of the transmission tunnel, and quite widely spaced. The instruments in front of the driver were to become synonymous with MGs – circular dials in a matt black facia. The overdrive switch was originally placed on the facia on the right-hand side. There was no interior light, merely a small map-reading lamp for the passenger. All-round visibility was good although the screen pillars were critized for their width. The lights were also good, save for the general comment that it was about time manufacturers fitted reversing lamps as standard.

The final comment from the 1966 road test was that the MGB GT was a smart newcomer from Abingdon that should go far and fast. The MGB did just that: more than half a million were built in the 18 years it was in production, a figure that needs no qualification – an all-time record for a British sports car.

Unfortunately, MG was never able to improve or replace the MGB as they wanted to, and by the 1970s the car was

Small back-seat drivers could be accommodated

The facia layout was to remain in MGBs for some time

GENERAL SPECIFICATION

Engine

Head/block	cast iron
Cylinders	4 in line
Bore/stroke	80·3 × 89 mm
Capacity	1,798 cc
Cooling	water
Valve gear	overhead pushrod
Compression	8·8:1
Carburettor	twin SU HS4
Max. power	95 bhp at 5,400 rpm
Max. torque	110 lb-ft at 3,000 rpm

Transmission

Type	4-speed manual, plus overdrive
Gear ratios	
Overdrive	0·80:1
Top	1·00:1
3rd	1·37:1
2nd	2·21:1
1st	3·64:1
Final drive	3·91:1

Suspension

Front	independent by coil springs, anti-roll bar
Rear	live axle, half-elliptic springs

Steering

Type	rack and pinion
Assistance	no

Brakes

Front	Lockheed 10¾-in disc
Rear	Lockheed 10-in drum
Servo	no

Wheels

Type	ventilated steel disc
Tyres	5·60–14 in

Electrical

Battery	12v, 58 a-h
Earth	positive
Dynamo	Lucas C40/1 (22 amp)

The tidily arranged engine compartment allowed for easy maintenance

really very out-of-date. There were improvements like all-synchromesh gearbox in 1967, and a reshaped facia from late 1974, but the most major change – certainly *not* an improvement – was the fitment of the large and controversial polyurethane bumpers and raised suspension necessary for continued American sales.

There was also the MGC, both in open and GT coupe form, for 1967. This was powered by the BMC six-cylinder 2·9 litre engine which gave the car a maximum speed of almost 120 mph but because of its increased weight, totally upset the car's handling. The MGB GT V8 was introduced in 1973, using the 3·5-litre Rover engine and giving the car a much needed performance boost and a top speed of 125 mph. This version really arrived too late, and as it could not be sold in MG's principle market, the USA, because of emission regulations, it was discontinued in 1976.

Despite becoming increasingly obsolete the MGB remained in production, even after its profitability disappeared. Rumours of the marque being 'bought' (at one time the name was linked with Aston Martin) all came to nothing and the protests of the MG supporters everywhere were finally silenced when Abingdon ceased MGB production in late 1980.

PERFORMANCE DATA
Date of test 4th March 1966

Maximum speeds	*mph*
Overdrive	98
Top	101
3rd	80
2nd	50
1st	30

Acceleration from rest	
mph	*sec*
0–30	4·8
0–40	6·2
0–50	9·3
0–60	13·6
0–70	19·0
0–80	25·4
0–90	38·1

Standing ¼ mile 19·1

Acceleration in	top	3rd
mph	*sec*	*sec*
10–30	—	8·1
20–40	11·1	7·0
30–50	10·8	7·1
40–60	10·8	7·6
50–70	12·6	8·4
60–80	15·3	11·6
70–90	20·4	—

Fuel consumption	
Overall	22·8 mpg
Tank capacity	12 gal.
Max. range	270 miles

Lotus Elan S4

Knowledge gained in the hard school of motor racing can benefit the ordinary production car, and this was especially true in the case of the Lotus Elan, which was a classic example of how racing design philosophy should be applied to a road going sports car. The Elan was in a class of its own in terms of performance and handling, without being in any way freakish.

The basic design changed little from the introduction of the Type 26 Elan in 1962. Foremost in the car's novel design features was Colin Chapman's steel backbone chassis, with the engine and gearbox between the front 'prong' and the transmission running along the boxed backbone. This avoided the need for the conventional tubular chassis that would otherwise have been necessary to support the glassfibre body.

The Elan S4 tested here was avilable in drophead and fixed head forms; both cost the same in 1969 – £1,353 in component form, or £1,769 for the completed car (inclusive of Purchase Tax). Our test car was fitted with a 3·77-to-1 final drive, which gave the car an overall gearing of 17·4 mph per 1,000 rpm.

Whereas the original Elans were fitted with the 1,498 cc Lotus twin-ohc conversion of the Ford 116E engine (developing 100 bhp at 5,700 rpm), models from 1963 onwards had the 1,558 cc Twin Cam race-bred engine, giving 115 bhp at 6,250 rpm. Initially this engine had a pair of Weber 40DCOE carburettors, until, in order to meet North American emission requirements Lotus abandoned the Webers in favour of Stromberg CD instruments. They claimed that other minor engine changes offset any power loss that resulted from this carburettor swap.

With its low weight and compact efficient shape, the Elan easily out-performed many of its bigger-engined rivals. With the hood up its maximum speed proved to be 124 mph. This was equivalent to 7,100 rpm, well above the engine's power peak. Even

The 1,558 cc engine was very flexible, and developed 115 bhp

The neat interior of the Elan, the instruments clearly visible for the driver

so, it was surprisingly smooth and certainly did not seem to object to the treatment.

Despite slightly lower gearing, this Elan's acceleration was not quite up to that of the earlier fixed-head model tested two years earlier. Nevertheless, its performance was still most impressive. From rest to 60 mph took only 7·8 sec which at the time was quicker than both a Porsche 911S and a Triumph TR6. With a sophisticated independent rear suspension layout and over 51 per cent of the kerb weight on the rear tyres, traction was exceptionally good and the little car simply rocketed away from the line, with a quarter mile time of only 15·9 sec.

Overall fuel consumption for the Elan of 30 mpg was streets ahead of the other cars in its class, typical comparisons being only 19·8 mpg for the Triumph TR6 and 21·8 mpg for the Jaguar E-type.

Full choke had to be used for cold starts, even in warm weather. Warm-up was reasonably quick but it was sometimes necessary to continue to use the choke

Both the spare wheel and the battery were housed in the boot

during this period. Once warm, idling was reasonable if a trifle lumpy. Throttle response was good while the delightful twin-cam engine was mechanically quiet and delightfully smooth. The water temperature gauge of our test car in warm weather frequently registered over 100 deg C in London traffic!

Clutch pedal travel felt just right and the amount of effort required was quite moderate. Take-up was a little abrupt, but this merely added to the precise feel of the controls. The gearbox was basically a Ford unit using the then-current Cortina GT ratios, which suited the Elan well.

Although the ride felt fairly firm at low speeds, it was by no means harsh. It felt considerably softer above 40 mph and became quite excellent at higher speeds. Very little road noise was transmitted into the car but there was a trace of scuttle shake on rough roads. High speeds over long undulations could produce sufficient rear suspension movement for the exhaust system to 'kiss' the road surface.

The rack-and-pinion steering was high geared (2·6 turns lock-to-lock) and was beautifully light, with a rapid response without being hypersensitive. Elan cornering was a revelation at the time. Many cars were capable of cornering fast, but the Elan instilled such confidence in the driver that at all normal speeds, the car simply went where it was pointed, with absolutely no fuss or drama. Pushed really hard, it would maintain the required tail-out attitude without any conscious effort on the driver's part. There was some body roll, but the occupants were scarcely aware of it. Apart from a tendency to squeal during braking, the Elan's behaviour on the road was excellent. The lot of the brakes (discs

GENERAL SPECIFICATION

Engine
Head/block	alloy/cast iron
Cylinders	4 in line
Bore/stroke	82·6 × 72·6 mm
Capacity	1,558 cc
Cooling	water
Valve gear	twin ohc
Compression	9·5:1
Carburettor	2 Stromberg 175CD2S
Max. power	115 bhp at 6,250 rpm
Max. torque	not available

Transmission
Type	4-speed manual
Gear ratios and mph/1,000 rpm	
Top	1·00:1/17·4
3rd	1·40:1/12·6
2nd	2·01:1/8·7
1st	2·97:1/5·9
Final drive	3·77:1

Suspension
Front	independent by coil springs, wishbones
Rear	independent by coil springs, wishbones

Steering
Type	rack and pinion
Assistance	no

Brakes
Front	Girling 10-in disc
Rear	Girling 10-in disc
Servo	yes

Wheels
Type	pressed-steel disc
Tyres	155–13 in

Electrical
Battery	12v, 57 a-h
Earth	positive
Dynamo	Lucas C40 (42 amp)
Headlamps	Lucas F700 120/90W

The compact, tidy shape of the Lotus Elan

PERFORMANCE DATA
Date of test 9th October 1969

Maximum speeds	mph	rpm
Top	124	7,100
3rd	90	7,200
2nd	62	7,200
1st	42	7,200

Acceleration from rest	
mph	sec
0–30	3·0
0–40	4·3
0–50	6·0
0–60	7·8
0–70	11·1
0–80	13·9
0–90	18·1
0–100	23·3
0–110	31·3

Acceleration in	top	3rd
mph	sec	sec
20–40	14·7	5·5
30–50	8·8	4·8
40–60	7·7	4·9
50–70	8·4	5·3
60–80	8·6	5·6
70–90	9·1	5·9
80–100	10·8	—
90–110	13·2	—

Fuel consumption	
Overall	30 mpg
Tank capacity	9·25 gal.
Max. range	275 miles

all round) was considerably eased as a result of the car's excellent handling.

Despite its small overall size, the Elan was surprisingly spacious. There was ample legroom and a small child could be accommodated in the rear without undue discomfort. The boot, although not large, was sensibly shaped and nicely trimmed. Considerable luggage could also be stowed behind the seats.

The erection and stowage of the hood was straightforward if somewhat fiddly. The hood fitted snugly and there was surprisingly little wind noise. The Elan had electric windows, which functioned well on the test car but were often to be the cause of reliability problems.

A fresh air, heating and ventilation system was provided, although temperature control was by a rather awkward knob that actuated a water valve. It could, however, get unpleasantly hot in an Elan in warm weather and the interior was prone to mist up on rainy days.

The Elan was a car for the open road – preferably a winding one – but it was also perfectly happy in traffic or pottering along country lanes. It offered a combination of performance, handling, economy and comfort that set standards that other manufacturers found hard to beat. Through its years of production their construction and finish improved, and when production ceased in 1973, 12,224 Elans had been built.

Lotus Seven Twin Cam SS

The Seven is a motoring anachronism. Still available 25 years after its introduction, it is an uncompromising sports car where performance and handling are *the* absolute priority.

Replacing Colin Chapman's first ever production car, the Six, in 1957 it was originally marketed as a kit car, thus allowing owners to avoid the addition of Purchase Tax on to the price. Its demise could have been heralded with Lotus' intention to go 'up-market' in the early 1970s. Fortunately, Caterham Cars, once a Lotus dealer, realized that the demand for the car would continue and they acquired the rights to build 'Caterham Sevens' in 1973. The Seven tested here, a 1970 Twin Cam SS, is therefore no longer strictly available, but thanks to Caterham Cars the Seven lives.

The orginal Lotus Seven first appeared at the 1957 London Motor Show, as a descendant of the successful club-racer, the Lotus Mark Six. Suspension was independent in front, using some Standard Triumph parts in a double wishbone and anti-roll bar layout, with a Ford live axle behind located by a shallow A-bracket and trailing arms; combined coil spring and damper units were used at each end. Steering was by rack and pinion, delightfully high-geared and tight locked, 2·7 turns for a 29½ ft turning circle between kerbs.

To make all this go, there was a Holbay-tuned Lotus-Ford twin ohc 1,558 cc engine which delivered 125 bhp at 6,200 rpm via a four-speed all-synchromesh gearbox and 3·9-to-1 final drive (with Hewland limited slip differential) to low-profile radial tyres and cast-alloy wheels. To make it stop there were Girling 9-in discs at the front, with drums at the rear. In spite of the engine being partly buried under the nose section

The Seven in its element – top down, on a windy country lane

(which had to be removed every time you needed to check the oil) weight distribution was only just front-heavy with no occupants and half a tank of fuel. With the tank filled (8 gallons) it was virtually 50-50.

With non-adjustable seats, the Lotus was best suited to drivers between 5 ft 8 in and 5 ft 10 in tall. With the hood down – the best way to drive it in *any* circumstances – taller drivers could get behind the wheel fairly easily, though knees were uncomfortably close to the wheel rim. Keen but tall drivers might have regretted that they are not made more welcome, but once in place all agreed the effort was worthwhile.

Both the rich mixture control for the two twin-choke 40DCOE Weber carburettors and the big button of the starter switch were hidden under the facia on the engine bulkhead. Starting was good, with the choke only needed for the first minute of running. Requiring a 50 lb shove, the Borg and Beck clutch was heavy. The short gear lever was extremely close to the wheel and had a positive, precise and sometimes slightly notchy action; in the main it was a delight.

The engine warmed-up quickly to around the indicated 90 deg C. There was a non-automatic electric fan for the radiator, but we never needed to switch it on, even in the heaviest traffic. Once it was warm, and if the road was clear, you were free to use the engine to its full.

As the performance figures show, the acceleration was fierce. In order to reduce one of the car's built-in headwinds slightly, performance measurements were taken with the hood up; that made little difference to the noise, which was dominated by the hard beat of the unsilenced induction trumpets and which became a snarl at high revs. Exhaust noise – a most unexpectedly lusty hiss not unlike that made by a contemporary Rolls-Royce accelerating flat-out – was only audible to bystanders. Standing starts were best made by feeding in the clutch at 4,500 rpm, which produced the least wheelspin, sometimes a little axle tramp and some snaking nearly all the way to 30 mph, 2·4 sec from rest; such take-offs achieved two-up (with test gear, a total of 358 lb payload) were extremely impressive and exciting. Brief wheelspin and a wiggle marked each hustled gearchange thereafter; 50 mph came up in 5·1 sec, 60 in 7·1 sec and 80 in 13·1 sec. Aerodynamic influences were felt overcoming the uncompromising body shape after 90 mph, reached in 18·8 sec with the top speed showing a mean 103 mph. One did of course pay for such performance in fuel consumption, which was a heavy 19 mpg (during the performance testing this dropped down to 15 mpg, which would have been typical if one had raced the car).

The engine was pretty flexible, pulling reasonably and without snatch from as little as 800 rpm. It began to get into its stride at around 3,500 rpm and really got going at 4,500 rpm all the way round to the red line at 6,500 rpm. This limit meant speeds in the closely spaced gears of 40, 58 and 84 mph, which was more than enough for most purposes. This was one of those cars where overtaking was made all the more easy and safer by the tremendous getaway. It was possible to over-do standing starts however, and during our acceleration runs the A-bracket that locates the rear axle buckled!

The impressive looking Twin Cam Lotus engine fills the 'under-bonnet' area

Following pages: In 1970, Lotus changed the Seven's looks with an 'almost' all-enveloping glassfibre body for the Mk IV version

With no boot, the Seven's spare wheel has to be strapped to the rear

Mean and purposeful. This car has its detachable sidescreens fitted

Cycle wings and free-standing headlights, not the most aerodynamic front end

Handling and roadholding were the Lotus Seven's other great virtues. Anyone used to cars with less accurate steering would tend to drive the Seven in a series of darts; there was virtually no free play and the effort needed at the wheel rim was low. After a while, directing the car became a mainly fingertip exercise, seemingly more mental than manual – until at the appropriate place, one started to corner at more than ordinary speeds. What little roll there was, was amplified visually by the wing tips. The car of course was basically an understeerer, although not to an unacceptable degree. If the road was smooth it took a great deal of power for the rear to break away, although it was not that difficult even on a good dry surface. On the track the true worth of the steering mechanism was apparent, which being high-geared and capable of large angles of lock enabled one to hold almost any slide one got into.

The car's security in handling was backed up by the brakes that did not fade at all. Pedal effort was akin to a racing car, abnormally high. The handbrake was a thing that you avoided using because of its awkward position under the facia on the passenger's side.

The Seven's ride was simply very firm. You watched out for the extra large potholes for the fear of the crashing noise that

GENERAL SPECIFICATION

Engine
Head/block	alloy/cast iron
Cylinders	4 in line
Bore/stroke	82·6 × 72·8 mm
Capacity	1,558 cc
Cooling	water
Valve gear	twin ohc
Compression	9·5:1
Carburettor	twin Weber DCOE twin-choke
Max. power	125 bhp at 6,200 rpm
Max. torque	116 lb-ft at 5,500 rpm

Transmission
Type	4-speed manual
Gear ratios	
Top	1·00:1
3rd	1·40:1
2nd	2·01:1
1st	2·97:1
Final drive	3·90:1 (limited slip differential)

Suspension
Front	independent by coil springs, double wishbones, anti-roll bar
Rear	live axle, coil springs, trailing arms, A-bracket

Steering
Type	rack and pinion
Assistance	no

Brakes
Front	Girling 9-in disc
Rear	Girling 8-in drum
Servo	no

Wheels
Type	cast alloy
Tyres	195–13 in

Electrical
Battery	12v, 39 a-h
Earth	negative
Dynamo	Lucas 42 amp
Headlamps	Lucas F700 120/90W

Just enough room for two. Note the small steering wheel and stubby gear lever

occurred every time you hit one – but this was acceptable as part of the car's character.

Seating was basic but not uncomfortable. You were located sideways simply by the cockpit wall and the side of the transmission tunnel. One was little more than elbow length away from the 13 in steering wheel.

Instrumentation was good, lacking only an oil temperature gauge, although this was not a problem with such a well cooled engine. Heater temperature was either hot or cold depending whether you had the blower fan on or off. Accelerator and brake pedals were well-placed for heel-and-toe changes, although the Seven badly needed a clutch foot-rest.

Erecting the hood, if really necessary, was somewhat laborious but not impossible, but by nature the Seven was a car you always drove with the hood down.

When Lotus decided to end the Seven's run, Caterham Cars bought the rights and have been building 'their' Sevens ever since. There are two Sevens available, one powered by the same Twin Cam engine as we tested in 1970, and a slightly 'tamer' version powered by a pushrod 1·6-litre Ford production engine.

1982 is the Seven's Jubilee year; hardly changed it remains a motoring experience in the true British sports car tradition.

PERFORMANCE DATA
Date of test 29th January 1970

Maximum speeds

	mph	rpm
Top	103	5,700
3rd	90	7,000
2nd	63	7,000
1st	43	7,000

Acceleration from rest

mph	sec
0–30	2·4
0–40	3·6
0–50	5·1
0–60	7·1
0–70	9·6
0–80	13·1
0–90	18·8

Standing ¼ mile 15·5

Acceleration in

mph	top sec	3rd sec
10–30	—	5·2
20–40	7·0	4·5
30–50	7·0	4·6
40–60	7·2	4·4
50–70	8·1	4·5
60–80	9·4	—
70–90	11·2	—

Fuel consumption

Overall	19·2 mpg
Tank capacity	8 gal.
Max. range	150 miles

Jensen-Healey

In the late 1960s Jensen, whilst doing a certain amount of contract work with other companies, only produced high-performance, expensive, executive cars. In order to survive, they had to expand. In 1970, a leading Californian sports car distributor, Kjell Qvale, led a consortium that bought their way into Jensen. With the demise of the Austin-Healey 3000, in 1968, enthusiasts were looking for a replacement – the demand for which was especially strong in the US, hence the American interest. With the appointment of Donald and Geoffrey Healey to the Jensen board, and financed by this new injection of American capital, the Jensen-Healey was born.

Bearing in mind all the background similarities and differences, it was amazing how closely the Jensen-Healey was cast in the Healey mould. Compared to the norm, the interval from the planning stage to full production, was very short indeed. The Jensen-Healey was aimed at a gap in the market for a good, value-for-money two-seater sports car. The unsuccessful replacement for the Healey 3000 had been the MGC, and the only comparable sports car around at the time were the MGB – acknowledged to be too slow – the little Midget, Triumph Spitfire and the TR6.

The new car was announced in March 1972 in time for the Geneva Motor Show. It was shown only as an open two seater, although a detachable hardtop was to be available as an extra. The body was made of steel, integral with a pressed platform chassis. The front and rear wings were bolted on for cheap and easy repair. As well as being dipped in primer, the body was

sprayed with bitumastic underseal on all exposed surfaces.

Suspension front and rear used Vauxhall Viva components, modified to provide significantly different geometry and with gas-filled dampers and shorter springs to give much better wheel control and the required ride height. Cast-alloy wheels with 5½J rims and low profile radial tyres were standard. Viva-type brakes were used with a large vacuum servo and special front pad material to balance the front/rear characteristics to the weight distribution of the car.

The engine was the then all-new 2-litre slant four built by Lotus; this had a die-cast aluminium block and head, twin overhead camshafts driven by a cogged rubber belt and was fed by twin Dellorto carburettors. In America, where the emission requirements were more stringent, twin Stromberg CD carburettors were used. Both engines had a compression ratio of 8·4-to-1, allowing them to run on only 91 octane (lead-free) fuel.

The Jensen-Healey weighed 19 cwt and was 20 per cent lighter than the Austin-Healey 3000 (which had a separate chassis). It developed 140 bhp at 6,500 rpm compared to the optimistic claim that the Mk III Healey 3000 developed 148 bhp at 5,350 rpm. The 92 in wheelbase was the same as the old Healey, but the body was 4½ in longer and 3 in wider. The front track was much better – always a weak point with the Healeys.

On acceleration, therefore, the Jensen-Healey was streets ahead of its predecessor, clocking 0-60 mph comfortably in under 8 sec. It was quicker than the Datsun 240Z, the Triumph TR6 (with fuel injection) and the Alfa Romeo 2000 GTV. On top speed it was ahead of most of its competitors, with the exception of the Datsun and the Alfa (both of which had the advantage of a five-speed gearbox).

It was not just in acceleration that the new engine impressed. In terms of flexibility and bottom-end pulling power it set an extraordinarily high standard. Potting along at only 20 mph in top, the car would pick up cleanly and quickly when the throttle was floored. The ease with which high gears could be used for brisk main road overtaking and the lusty way the engine pulled so strongly all the time created a great impression.

Starting was at all times instantaneous, a little choke first thing in the morning being all that was needed. Immediately the knob

could be pushed back, the engine able to run smoothly without hesitation, throttle response always immediate and clean.

Clutch effort was pleasantly light and the pedal action well designed for easy and progressive action. The clutch was notable for its pleasant characteristics, with the Chrysler gearbox equipped with powerful synchromesh and well-spaced ratios, indirect maxima were 41, 64 and 98 mph at 7,000 rpm.

The Jensen-Healey lagged a little behind the Lotus Elan on outright performance, although it more than made up for this in terms of ride. For a sports car the ride was definitely soft. Main road bumps were soaked up extremely well by the generous wheel travel and supple suspension.

The rack and pinion steering was very light, even when parking in a tight spot. With just over three turns from lock to lock, it was about right for driving around town,

and with little more than a flick of the wrist needed to change lanes at speed on a motorway.

When cornering there seemed to be almost unlimited front end grip. Towards the limit there was some understeer, which became progressively stronger until the front end ran wide of the chosen radius, but this behaviour was well outside the normal course of driving on public roads.

The light and progressive brakes had plenty of 'bite', being perfect to match the car's performance.

Unlike many other sports cars, the Jensen-Healey was built for drivers with long legs and big feet. It was possible to get well back from the pedals which were well spaced and had a wide clear area to rest the left foot when it was off the clutch. Seat comfort was good, the combination of firmness for lateral support and softness for extra bump absorption was well balanced. Small head restraints were standard, and they did not restrict visibility in any way.

In front of the driver the oval instrument panel contained matching speedometer and rev counter, flanked by clearly visible oil pressure and water temperature gauges. Outboard of these were the fuel gauge and battery voltmeter, both somewhat obscured by the driver's hands. Two small sub panels flanked the steering column on the lower edge of the facia, containing rocker switches for lamp and hazard warning, on one side and the other side blank for any necessary accessory switches.

The hood itself was a neat piece of tailoring, only taking a few minutes to fold away or put up. The unframed side windows fitted snugly against the hood apertures, and were draught free.

A General Motors collapsible steering column was fitted, together with a Vauxhall-type steering lock which required two hands to operate it, and remove the key. The boot was a reasonable size for a sports car, the shape being sensibly square to take suitcases and squashy holdalls. The spare wheel was housed in a cradle underneath

The Lotus engine with twin Dellorto carburettors developed 140 bhp

GENERAL SPECIFICATION

Engine
Head/block	alloy
Cylinders	4 in line
Bore/stroke	95·2 × 69·3 mm
Capacity	1,973 cc
Cooling	water
Valve gear	twin ohc
Compression	8·4:1
Carburettor	2 Dellorto DHLA40
Max. power	140 bhp at 6,500 rpm
Max. torque	130 lb-ft at 5,000 rpm

Transmission
Type	4-speed manual
Gear ratios	
Top	1·00:1
3rd	1·29:1
2nd	1·99:1
1st	3·12:1
Final drive	3·73:1

Suspension
Front	independent by coil springs, wishbones
Rear	live axle, coil springs, trailing and semi-trailing links

Steering
Type	rack and pinion
Assistance	no

Brakes
Front	Girling 10-in disc
Rear	Lockheed 9-in drum
Servo	Girling

Wheels
Type	cast alloy
Tyres	185/70HR–13 in

Electrical
Battery	12v, 50 a-h
Earth	negative
Alternator	AC-Delco, 35 amp
Headlamps	Lucas sealed 150/100W

The plain but purposeful interior

the boot, and was winched down with a wheelbrace.

The bonnet lid extended the full width between the front wing crowns, which provided excellent accessibility to the engine, although the slant of the engine made any work on the distributor almost impossible.

The 1972 price for a new Jensen-Healey was £1,810, and was thought to be pitched at just the right market to compete with home-built offerings from British Leyland and the imported opposition from Alfa Romeo and Datsun. In that particular segment of the market it had little opposition, and in the beginning home sale prospects looked very good. Overseas it was thought that it would have to fight a little harder for sales, but in all the important characteristics of handling, ride and comfort it came out very well. Unfortunately, the Jensen-Healey soon showed that it lacked development, many of the early cars were unreliable. So the car gained a bad reputation, and when the oil crisis in the mid-1970s threatened the financial base of Jensen – and the Government refused aid – the Receiver was called in and the company was wound up in 1976.

Time has forgiven the Jensen-Healey some of its faults, and the qualities that were so appealing when the car was launched in the spring of 1972 have made it a collector's item, a classic car in the mould of its esteemed predecessor.

PERFORMANCE DATA
Date of test 31st August 1972

Maximum speeds	*mph*	*rpm*
Top	119	6,600
3rd	98	7,000
2nd	64	7,000
1st	41	7,000

Acceleration from rest	
mph	*sec*
0–30	2·8
0–40	4·2
0–50	5·9
0–60	7·8
0–70	10·9
0–80	14·3
0–90	18·7
0–100	24·7
0–110	36·0

Standing ¼ mile		16·2

Acceleration in	top	3rd
mph	*sec*	*sec*
10–30	—	7·2
20–40	7·9	5·9
30–50	7·8	5·6
40–60	8·1	5·6
50–70	8·4	5·8
70–90	8·7	6·2
80–100	9·7	7·4
90–110	11·7	—
100–120	17·8	—

Fuel consumption	
Overall	24 mpg
Tank capacity	11 gal.
Max. range	260 miles

Reliant Scimitar GTE

Reliant was already well-known for 'three-wheeler' economy cars when the first four-wheeled sports car was introduced in 1961. In various forms the Reliant Sabre and the Sabre Six continued into the mid-1960s, when they were replaced by the 3-litre Scimitar. David Ogle's design was unveiled at the 1967 Motor Show in London and created a favourable impression.

The Tamworth firm's first major development of the design was the GTE version of the Scimitar that came along in 1969. The GTE kept the Ogle Scimitar front end but was completely restyled at the rear to offer four-seater accommodation and increased luggage space whilst remaining a sports car. Within three years, in response to demand, the fixed-head coupe version was discontinued and Reliant concentrated on this practical GT estate car.

From the outset the GTE was powered by the Ford V6 3-litre engine. In late 1971 Ford increased the power output of this engine (used in the Capri) from 127 bhp to 138 bhp and at the same time substituted a German-made manual gearbox with closer indirect ratios. This left Reliant with something of a dilemma. The new close ratio gearbox could not take an overdrive, which had been a standard feature on previous manual Scimitars, and which was an essential part of the GTE's character. The solution was to offer a choice of manual transmissions, the 'old' gearbox with overdrive and the new one without it. When the overdrive combination was not fitted, a 3·07-to-1 final drive ratio was provided in place of the 3·31-to-1 with overdrive. The difference in the overall gearing for cruising was not therefore significantly reduced without the overdrive, from 26·8 to 23·7 mph per 1,000 rpm in fact.

In a car like this, high gearing did not necessarily mean that the step-off performance would be reduced, and this manual GTE proved quicker to 90 mph than the overdrive version. On the road one used the gearbox more than with the overdrive version, largely because the really 'long' lower ratios were so useful. At 6,000 rpm in third the manual GTE recorded 103 mph, which made it an excellent gear for almost any sort of overtaking even on motorways, in keeping with the Scimitar's character.

Probably the car's most distinctive angle

The spare wheel was positioned in the engine bay to save space and to act as a 'shock absorber' in a major frontal collision

Enrichment when cold was automatic and the engine warmed quickly to a smooth tickover. The engine felt very refined up to 4,000 rpm, but when called to work hard it became quite harsh, especially at the top end. Top speed was recorded slightly over the top of the engine's power curve, as 121 mph at 5,100 rpm.

Clutch effort was not heavy by sports car standards, but the pedal travel was rather long, which was irksome in traffic, especially as full release was necessary for easy shifting. The gearchange was positive, with effective synchromesh making down-changes to first gear very easy.

Coil springs were used all round for the suspension, but although this was independent by wishbones at the front, at the rear there was a live rear axle located by parallel trailing arms with Watts linkage. The suspension was very firm, but well damped and coped with poor roads with surprisingly little discomfort. On secondary roads there was a lot of jogging movement accentuated by the fairly hard upholstery used in the seats. In the style of many GT cars of the time, the ride firmness was shaken off as speed rose, with the car becoming pleasantly comfortable on a motorway.

Steering was by rack and pinion, giving good sensitivity and accurate response to small movements of the wheel. Quite heavy when pulling the car through tight bends, it was even worse at manoeuvring speeds and coupled with a 37 ft turning circle it made parking something of a struggle (later models were fitted with power steering).

When cornering hard there was little roll, just a slight lean as the car took its line, and with power applied in the right gear the tail followed round nicely, giving a pleasantly well-balanced feel to the handling. Girling discs were used at the front, with drums at

Leather seats were an optional extra. In front of the driver, a comprehensive display of instruments

the rear, and response was good. Coupled with the general handling characteristics of the car a reassuring feeling of confidence and security was transmitted to the driver.

Upholstery was normally in pvc with leather available as an extra, at a cost in 1973 of £40. The seat backrests were somewhat diminutive, but were comfortable and gave a reasonable degree of lateral location. The car was a true four-seater, with snug rear seats and adequate headroom, although leg space was somewhat limited. The headlining in black cloth was practical but tended to give the interior a rather sombre nature. Centre armrests were fitted front and back, the latter tipping forward and acting as a luggage stop when the car was being used as a two-seater estate.

The GTE was designed as a long-range touring car, and its 17 gallon fuel tank allowed for 400 miles between fill-ups.

The spare wheel was mounted in the front of the engine compartment, secured by a large T-handle bolt through one of the wheel studs. It was quite a struggle to remove it, but its position meant increased space in the rear of the car for extra luggage

The GTE offered quite reasonable comfort for rear seat passengers

GENERAL SPECIFICATION

Engine
Head/block	cast iron
Cylinders	6 in 60° vee
Bore/stroke	93·67 × 72·42 mm
Capacity	2,994 cc
Cooling	water
Valve gear	overhead pushrod
Compression	8·9:1
Carburettor	Weber 40DFA progressive choke
Max. power	138 bhp at 5,000 rpm
Max. torque	172 lb-ft at 3,000 rpm

Transmission
Type	4-speed manual
Gear ratios	
Top	1·00:1
3rd	1·41:1
2nd	1·95:1
1st	3·16:1
Final drive	3·07:1

Suspension
Front	independent by coil springs, wishbones, anti-roll bar
Rear	live axle, trailing arms, Watts linkage, coil springs, anti-roll bar

Steering
Type	rack and pinion
Assistance	no

Brakes
Front	Girling 10·63-in disc
Rear	Girling 9-in drum
Servo	yes

Wheels
Type	pressed-steel disc
Tyres	185HR–14 in

Electrical
Battery	12v, 55 a-h
Earth	negative
Alternator	Lucas 11AC 35 amp
Headlamps	150/120

The car was a high-speed hatchback with impressive load capacity

space and extra tank capacity. It also offered a good safety factor in a frontal accident.

The arrangement for turning the rear compartment into a load carrier was excellent, and although there was a fairly high sill at the back over which luggage had to be lifted, the opening was reasonably deep and the back window hatch was held open by gas-strut. The rear seats were easily folded forward, providing the car with a large, flat load area. A considerable amount could be carried by the Scimitar, with a maximum payload of 950 lb.

Access to the rear seats was easy for anyone who was reasonably active, with grab handles on each side to help.

Not least of the Scimitar's advantages was the massive steel box-section chassis and glassfibre body which promised extended life free from corrosion. The GTE offered adequate accommodation for four, a high standard of safety and was suitable for all who wanted a practical fast 'GT estate sports car'.

The GTE set a new fashion for a kind of strongly sports-accented estate car – a good attempt to comfort that traditional figure of motoring irony, the sports car bachelor who marries and must later surrender his two-seater with the advent of a young family. The GTE was listed through the 1970s, available in manual or automatic guise, and in 1980 it was further developed. The GTC was an attempt to fill the gap left by the demise of the Triumph Stag, as a genuine four-seater convertible. It has a T-shaped roll-over bar similar to the Stag's, which to many eyes makes the car even more appealing with the only real drawback being the loss of some of the car's utility. Reliant still offer two contrasting motoring styles from the sporting GTE and GTCs down to the very economical three-wheeled Rialto and four-wheeled Kitten estate.

PERFORMANCE DATA
Date of test 1st Feburary 1973

Maximum speeds *mph* *rpm*

	mph	rpm
Top	121	5,100
3rd	103	6,000
2nd	73	6,000
1st	45	6,000

Acceleration from rest

mph	sec
0–30	3·0
0–40	4·4
0–50	6·4
0–60	8·9
0–70	11·8
0–80	15·8
0–90	20·5
0–100	28·1
0–110	39·5

Standing ¼ mile 16·9

Acceleration in

mph	top sec	3rd sec
10–30	—	6·7
20–40	9·9	6·2
30–50	9·1	6·0
40–60	9·2	6·1
50–70	10·1	6·3
60–80	10·8	6·8
70–90	12·2	8·2
80–100	14·5	11·1
90–110	19·3	—

Fuel consumption
Overall 24 mpg
Tank capacity 17 gal.
Max. range 400 miles

Jaguar E-type V12

When the Jaguar E-type was unveiled in 1961 it was as advanced as the XK120 had been 13 years before. A striking descendant, it followed the Jaguar tradition and was rightly acclaimed as 'sensational'. The separate chassis of the XK had been replaced by a stressed-steel monocoque, like the D-type sports-racing car it resembled, but with all-round independent suspension.

The E-type was a yardstick by which other cars were measured. It reached unparalleled performance and outstanding value for money in 1971 when the Series 3 versions were introduced with Jaguar's 5·3-litre V12 engine and a slightly increased wheelbase.

At this time, there was a distinct paucity of open sports cars on the British market. With the disappearance from this segment of the market of Ferrari (apart from the Dino Spider), Maserati and Aston Martin, the choice was narrowed considerably. It was left to Jaguar to uphold the honour of the quality open top sports car and the E-type in its Series 3 form set undeniably high standards in a shrinking field. Fears that forthcoming American regulations would ban open cars forever (although unfounded), could not colour the joys of open air motoring in considerable luxury offered by the E-type.

To those people who thought that a sports car should have a bone hard ride, a glorious exhaust note and a draughty hood on a frame – some people still do – the V12 Roadster was probably a considerable disappointment, for in all these departments the car was highly refined. In no way could driving the car be considered an adventure in the traditional idiom.

Despite the increase in the E-type's capacity of more than 40 per cent since its introduction (the Series 1 had the Jaguar straight six 3·8-litre engine), the ultimate performance of the car changed very little. This was partly due to the steady increase in overall weight, for the Series 3 car was no less than 22 per cent heavier than the original model. Very little of this increase could be put down to the V12 engine, because it was largely made from aluminium alloy and weighed only 65 lb more than the cast-iron XK series straight six. Most of the weight was from the extra furnishings and equipment.

It was logical that the V12 Roadster should share the long-wheelbase chassis of the Coupe and this provided a welcome increase in the amount of interior stowage space.

For maximum speed runs in the test and for continuous speeds in excess of 120 mph the tyre pressures were raised to the

The attractive and distinctive shape of the E-type

prescribed 40 psi. At this pressure, the ride at slow speed was extremely harsh, but it was thought best to put up with this slow speed harshness to allow high cruising speeds when conditions permitted. The maximum speed of our test car was 143 mph, the engine revving at 6,200 rpm. This speed could be held without temperament for several miles, and the car felt rock steady, although the combination of tyre and wind roar was high.

The performance of the V12 Roadster was impressive by any standards. A car that only takes six seconds for each 20 mph increment from 20 to 90 mph is very fast, and the smooth ease with which the Jaguar achieved this was most impressive. As a further demonstration of the remarkable flexibility of the engine, the V12 proved capable of accelerating from rest to 110 mph in top gear in 36·4 sec. In practice this meant that rapid progress could be made without continuous use of the gearbox, contributing to the relaxed enjoyment of the car.

The deceptive way in which the power was delivered, and the low level of noise, except at high speeds, meant that it was an easy car to misjudge speeds. There was little increase of the exhaust note and even with the hood down, in a narrow high-walled street the most one heard was a pleasant musical hum from the exhaust. There was very little whine from the camshaft chains but at very high revs with the hood down an exciting chatter, rising to a deepthroated thrum, could be heard from the valve gear. At no time could any induction roar be heard.

The turbine-like smoothness with which the engine provided a sustained shove in the back was almost uncanny, the more so when accelerating hard in top gear without even a gear change to interrupt the dramatic rise in speed.

It was perhaps as well that limited use was made of the gearbox, for although the all-synchromesh unit that was introduced in 1964 worked well, the change was not particularly quick, and the movement between the gears was long.

Despite what was, in 1971, an advanced design, the engine was not as efficient in terms of fuel economy as the old XK series, and even the most careful use of the accelerator could not give better than 16 to 17 mpg.

Power steering offered the right amount of assistance to relieve the tedium of parking or low speed manoeuvring, while at speed, stability and precision was excellent. Steering response was quick, with road shocks well insulated.

The car's not inconsiderable weight was almost perfectly distributed 50:50 and it felt extremely well balanced. Such balance when allied to the grip of the Dunlop SP

Top: The smooth and refined V12 engine

Above: The familiar Jaguar facia. Note that the bulge in the bonnet was no longer strictly necessary

Sport tyres meant that it was extremely difficult to break adhesion at either end. There was little trace of roll, and in most conditions the car went where it was pointed. In the wet, the grip was also excellent, but some caution was needed on really slippery roads, as the engine was capable of pouring out the torque so smoothly that wheelspin would occur at remarkably low speeds. Anti-dive characteristics were introduced to the front suspension, which effectively limited the dipping of the nose under heavy braking.

The brakes were perhaps the poorest feature on both the Series 1 and 2 E-types, but those on the Series 3 V12 were beyond criticism. Response and anti-fade characteristics were as one would expect in a car of this nature, with the effort needed for check braking pleasantly light and progressive.

The leather seats were comfortable and the control of the rake adequately fine. Much valuable room was gained behind the seats by the use of the long-wheelbase chassis, and the space above the differential nose had a useful locker, running the whole width of the car. The seating position was good, with the full complement of instruments laid out in front of the driver. The steering wheel was adjustable for reach. Power steering allowed a small diameter wheel to be used.

The adoption of the more steeply-sloped windscreen of the long-wheelbase Series 3 meant the disappearance of the three wiper set-up, the two blades were able to sweep the wide screen well, leaving only two blind spots at the extreme edges of the screen, where it curved round to meet the side windows. Visibility was good at the front and sides, although three-quarter vision was restricted with the hood up.

The 1973 price of the test car, £3,711, included a number of desirable extras, and represented outstanding value for money. The hard top was a most substantial and well-finished affair, two people being required to fit, or remove it. In winter, the hard top allowed the car to revert to its role as a closed coupe, and the built-in vents gave useful air extraction, lacking in the hood. The hood itself was also well-made,

Most of the boot space was taken up by the spare wheel and tool kit

GENERAL SPECIFICATION

Engine
Head/block	alloy
Cylinders	12 in 60° vee
Bore/stroke	90 × 70 mm
Capacity	5,343 cc
Cooling	water
Valve gear	sohc per bank
Compression	9:1
Carburettor	4 Stromberg 175CDSE
Max. power	266 bhp at 5,750 rpm
Max. torque	304 lb-ft at 3,500 rpm

Transmission
Type	4-speed manual
Gear ratios	
Top	1·000:1
3rd	1·389:1
2nd	1·905:1
1st	2·933:1
Final drive	3·310:1

Suspension
Front	independent by wishbones, torsion bars, anti-roll bar
Rear	independent by coil springs, lower wishbones, radius arms, anti-roll bar

Steering
Type	rack and pinion
Assistance	yes

Brakes
Front	Girling 11·18-in ventilated disc
Rear	Girling 10·38-in ventilated disc
Servo	yes

Wheels
Type	ventilated steel disc
Tyres	E70VR–15 in

Electrical
Battery	12v, 60 a-h
Earth	negative
Alternator	Butec A7/1A, 60 amp
Headlamps	Cibie Biode 220/110W

Even with the hood erected the E-type has superb lines

but not as simple to raise and lower as in previous models.

Most of the items under the bonnet requiring regular attention were readily accessible, although a Jaguar V12 engine was – indeed remains – no easy task for the average enthusiastic DIY home mechanic; the impressive sight under the bonnet was generally left to the more experienced to service.

Over 15,000 V12 Jaguars were built out of a total E-type production run of 75,584. The E-type fully reflected William Lyons' philosophy of value for money and exceptional engineering quality. The E-type represented a standard – often sought after but seldom achieved – for an entire breed of sports car. They remain superb, striking sports cars.

There was a useful compartment behind the seats

PERFORMANCE DATA
Date of test 5th July 1973

Maximum speeds	mph	rpm
Top	143	6,200
3rd	108	6,500
2nd	78	6,500
1st	52	6,500

Acceleration from rest	
mph	sec
0–30	2·6
0–40	3·8
0–50	5·2
0–60	7·2
0–70	9·2
0–80	11·8
0–90	14·9
0–100	18·4
0–110	24·2
0–120	32·5

Standing ¼ mile		15·1

Acceleration in	top	3rd
mph	sec	sec
10–30	6·7	4·4
20–40	5·8	3·7
30–50	5·4	3·7
40–60	5·4	3·7
50–70	5·4	3·8
60–80	5·4	4·3
70–90	5·9	5·0
80–100	6·8	6·3
90–110	8·8	9·0
100–120	15·3	—

Fuel consumption	
Overall	16 mpg
Tank capacity	18 gal.
Max. range	280 miles

Morgan Plus 8

Morgan have been making cars since 1910, and the only real change since then has been the addition of a fourth wheel. Morgan made their spritely three-wheelers until 1936, then turned to *real* cars, producing the Morgan 4/4 (four wheels/four cylinders). These traditionally styled cars have kept their pre-war design to the present day, and will continue to do so while the order book remains full, measured in years rather than months.

The most exciting of all Morgans is the Plus 8 which made its debut at the 1968 London Motor Show. The Plus 8 is the most outrageous survivor of the Morgan brood, using the Rover 3½-litre V8 engine to drive a ladder chassis based on a pair of torsionally whippy cross-braced Z-section members, with most of the body framing carried out in ash, laminated or plain. Thanks to the low weight of the light-alloy engine, the car scales only 2,310 lb in the standard steel-panelled version.

In 1973 the Plus 8 was given the Rover five-speed overdrive gearbox, the original gearbox was the famous old Moss Gears four-speed unit, a distinctly character-full box that worked well enough when you had been reminded of the lack of any synchromesh on first and not much on the upper three gears.

Using the Rover gearbox has done away with the short cast torque tube separating the Moss box from the back of the engine, and brought the engine itself a little further back. The Rover transmission has a 1-to-1 fourth gear and a 0·834 top.

The performance of the Plus 8 is very exhilerating. 30 mph is reached in 2·2 sec, 50 in 4·6, 60 in 6·5, 80 in 11·4, and 100 mph in 20·2 sec and a final top speed of 123 mph. The gearbox has nicely spaced ratios, with a superb gearchange quality – light precise, short of excess movement and always a delight, and in contrast to the very stiff original Moss four-speed unit, there is

also a very reliable synchromesh on all forward gears.

Enough of figures for the moment; one must attempt to describe the tremendously satisfying performances of the car. The standing starts were sheer wanton pleasure – drop the clutch in at 3,000 rpm, and the limited slip differential encourages both big rear wheels to scream with spin most of the way to that excellent 2·2 sec 30 mph time. Bang the lever through into second and there is another yelp as the car leaps forward yet again.

We have tested cars with faster times, but no more exciting than the Plus 8.

The Rover's effortless 198 lb-ft of torque – at only 2,500 rpm – and its 155 bhp mean magnificent flexibility and super top gear acceleration, with instant pick-up at all times. In town you burble off the line in first, and plop it into top at 30.

You are certainly conscious of the engine's exhaust note from the two pipes, deep-voiced behind. It is easier than in many sporting cars to pass through inhabited places quietly in the Morgan, thanks to that flexibility. You can make yourself very audible, if you must, by opening the beautifully progressively, traditional roller-pedalled throttle – but there is no need for such crass behaviour where it might cause offence. There is also the clear clicking of the electric fuel pump behind your head; you hear that at town speeds too. At anything from 50 mph onwards with the hood up, wind noise grows to well-high appalling levels – it is a screaming hiss above 110 which is almost intolerable.

The handling of the Morgan is inextricably bound up with the ride. Cam Gears worm and nut steering is used, and is high geared, needing only 2·4 turns lock to lock for a 39 ft 11 in. mean turning circle. It seems paradoxical that a sports car whose purpose is better agility, should have a restricted lock, but it has long been so in this case. Fortunately, the design of the car forces the driver to sit relatively close to the wheel, which helps him provide the muscle needed to steer at low speeds – and indeed at very high ones when cornering; steering effort is great enough when rounding a bend at the very high rates of which the car is capable for one to wish that the steering wheel spokes were made smoother near the rim.

There is plenty of feel, rapid self-centring, some (but not too much) kick-back, and quick response. There is also some perceptible play about the straight ahead, roughly 1 in at the rim. The weight of the steering makes fast corners excessively hard work, which is a pity because the car's smooth road limit is very high. It rolls very little. It is slightly more rear-biased in weight distribution – 47·4/52·6 against 48·1/51·9 front/rear thanks to the new engine position – yet there is some marked understeer due partly one suspects to the limited-slip differential. It is very hard to make it break away behind even using all that 137 bhp/ton laden power-to-weight ratio – on smooth roads. Hit a bump, even quite a small bump, and the

The heart of the matter – the bonnet hinges in the middle to reveal the Rover V8 engine

The tonneau cover allows the driver to travel with the top down even in cold weather

105

rear axle hops out readily, sometimes setting the back sliding if there's enough power on, at other times simply making the car wriggle sharply.

Obviously, the Morgan hop-steers, considerably and often, when so many roads even in Britain have bumps. On a few occasions, we also encountered some chassis-steer – true bump-steer – when a road irregularity made the car weave surprisingly. It is a handful down a country road – not dangerous by any means, because in spite of its waywardnesses, it is essentially very stable and will always put itself right – but you have to work hard. And of course the problem is mainly the ride, which is simply very bumpy. At the front the famous Morgan sliding pillar independent suspension allows $2\frac{1}{4}$ in bump, $1\frac{7}{8}$ in rebound. Behind the movement range of the short half-elliptics is $3\frac{3}{4}$ in/1 in. The result is an understandably violent ride which is something else by modern standards. You can argue that over many roads, the Morgan gets away with it adequately, which is quite true. After a while one takes pleasure in the stirring way the Plus 8 sweeps over open roads – the striding longleggedness of the gearing and the always confident power allied to the short sharp pitches of the ride together translate into a wonderful bounding motion. But hit a heavier bump at speed, and there is a crash from behind as the axle hits something, you bounce up in the seat – if the hood is up, your head sometimes hits a hood stick – and the car bucks itself briefly askew, wriggling straight again. There are bumps on some motorways which will do this sort of thing to the Plus 8 at high speed.

The Morgan is, however, inherently stable. There are no dangers in its suspension geometry which can build up into something out-of-hand after bump-induced instability. You can say it is fun, which it is; Morgan explain that they do not have the slightest intention of competing with the mass sports-car market.

The disc/drum servo-assisted brake layout works well. The handbrake of the Plus 8 is applied by the delightful fly-off lever. A fly-off handbrake is in effect a conventional handbrake with the spring

The controls are simple, in traditional style

GENERAL SPECIFICATION

Engine
Head/block	alloy
Cylinders	8 in 90° vee
Bore/stroke	88·9 × 71·12 mm
Capacity	3,532 cc
Cooling	water
Valve gear	overhead pushrod
Compression	9·35:1
Carburettor	twin SU HIF6
Max. power	155 bhp at 5,250 rpm
Max. torque	198 lb-ft at 2,500 rpm

Transmission
Type	5-speed manual
Gear ratios and mph/1,000 rpm	
Top	0·834:1/26·2
4th	1·000:1/21·84
3rd	1·396:1/15·65
2nd	2·085:1/10·48
1st	3·320:1/6·58
Final drive	3·310:1

Suspension
Front	independent by coil springs, sliding pillar and leaf springs
Rear	live axle, leaf springs

Steering
Type	Cam Gears worm and nut
Assistance	no

Brakes
Front	Girling 11-in disc
Rear	Girling 9-in drum
Servo	yes

Wheels
Type	cast light alloy
Tyres	185/70VR–14 in

Electrical
Battery	12v, 57 a-h
Earth	negative
Alternator	Lucas 11AC 45 amp
Headlamps	120/90W

holding the release pawl in the ratchet working gently in the opposite direction. To set the brake, you pull it back and press the top down (which engages the pawl); to release it, you simply pull the lever back briefly and let go – hence fly-off.

You sit close to the wheel in the Morgan. There is just enough rearward movement of the seat to enable a six-foot driver to make himself comfortable. The pedals are ideally placed for heel-and-toe changes. The view out over the bonnet is impressive, the lines of louvres tapering towards the front, emphasizing the perspective. With the hood up, there are serious blind spots, just behind one's shoulder, but the rear view is excellent.

Looking through the windscreen you see three windscreen wiper arms, toy-like in their proportions, but they clean the screen well, leaving little unswept.

Underbonnet space is crowded by the handsome V8 engine, and for certain work one is thankful with the ease in which the traditional side opening bonnet can be removed.

It is easy to see why the Morgan Plus 8 has such a devoted following. Mechanically it is a superb sports car, providing magnificent performance up to 100 mph; the fact that the built-in headwinds slow it appreciably after that does not matter much. Most of us would not want the shape changed; and with a full order book even today, it is unlikely that they ever will.

PERFORMANCE DATA
Date of test 15th July 1978

Maximum speeds	mph	rpm
Top	123	4,700
4th	121	4,750
3rd	94	6,000
2nd	63	6,000
1st	40	6,000

Acceleration from rest	sec
0–30	2·2
0–40	3·5
0–50	4·6
0–60	6·5
0–70	9·0
0–80	11·4
0–90	15·4
0–100	20·2
0–110	31·0

Standing ¼ mile	15·1

Acceleration in	top	4th
mph	sec	sec
10–30	8·8	6·4
20–40	7·7	5·6
30–50	6·8	4·9
40–60	6·7	4·9
50–70	7·2	5·2
60–80	7·9	5·7
70–90	9·2	6·9
80–100	11·8	8·6
90–100	20·3	12·6

Fuel consumption
Overall   20·5 mpg
Tank capacity 14 gal.
Max. range   280 miles

Triumph TR7 Drophead

It was bad news for Britain, when in 1970, America apparently decided to ban convertibles in forthcoming crash and rollover safety regulations, and the future of our sports cars looked doomed. Then came the reprieve – open cars were not to be banned after all; but by then the Triumph TR7 had been designed specifically as a closed top coupe version only.

To start with a car designed only for a closed top, and convert it to an open version is not as easy as when the whole concept is tackled at the design stage. Hence there was considerable delay in the introduction of the TR7 Drophead. The original coupe version was introduced to the UK in September 1975, the open top version arrived five years later in early 1980.

The wedge-shaped appearance of the coupe was often criticized, whereas the open Drophead was much better received. It achieved a degree of simplicity of styling in spite of the heavy bumpers required for American safety regulations.

Those shapely lines and swept back windscreen would have looked rather silly if the TR7 had not had the performance they implied. Good spacing of the gear ratios, however, allowed drivers to make full use of the power available, with the 2-litre Dolomite engine having a wide range of useful revs, pulling strongly and smoothly from about 1,500 rpm to 5,500 rpm.

When tested, the Drophead reached 60 mph in 10·7 sec, covered the standing quarter-mile in 18·1 sec and went to 100 mph in 42·0 sec from rest. The Drophead was given a slightly lower fourth gear than the previous model, having a 3·9-to-1 final drive ratio instead of 3·63; but in fifth, of course, it was much higher geared and gave a long-legged feel. At the 6,500 rpm limit, maximum speed in first, second and third gears were recorded as 34, 54 and 80 mph respectively. In fifth gear the maximum could be affected by wind or a slight gradient, but our mean maximum came to 114 mph.

Originally designed as a fixed-head coupe, many felt the TR7 was better looking as a Drophead

The gearchange was ideally placed for the driver's left hand to fall naturally from the wheel straight on to it, and was light and smooth in action. Clutch action appeared pleasantly light, with short travel and progressive take up, making it easy to move smoothly off from rest.

The sporting nature of the Drophead made the noise level reasonably acceptable. Much of the noise was wind roar, which built up over 80 mph. At lower speeds the engine sounded crisp and smooth.

The eager character of the TR7 Drophead, even with the fifth gear and the very efficient Triumph ohc 2-litre engine with twin SU carburettors, led to an overall test fuel consumption of 25 mpg. The 12 gallon tank allowed a range of 250 miles before the fuel warning light came on.

The heavyweight bias at the front of the TR7 Drophead gave it quite a marked understeer, and the cornering behaviour was consistant and reassuring until the car was pushed hard. On an uneven surface the limitations of a live rear axle tended to be noticed, when the rear wheels were prone to skitter outwards on a hard corner. Even when cornering hard, body roll was to a minimum, helped by the anti-roll bars at each end. The MacPherson strut front suspension and live rear axle located by trailing and semi-trailing arms, gave an impressively good ride comfort with the right degree of firmness and good absorption of bumps and undulations on indifferent secondary roads.

It is often a problem with an open car that the structure may feel weak, with violent shake on bad roads. The TR7 Drophead resisted that well, feeling all in one strong piece even when bad bumps were hit at speed. Much of the charm of the TR's road behaviour was derived from the car's impeccable steering, with precise control responding to the tiniest movement of the wheel. Light when on the move, the steering tended to tighten at parking speeds, but even then the turning circle of only 29½ ft helped when parking in tight spaces.

The Lockheed disc brakes at the front and drums at the rear were servo-assisted, and gave progressive response up to a point where the front wheels were prone to lock, producing a slight slewing movement and thus imposing a rather low limit of stopping ability. We felt the rear brakes were not trying hard enough.

Our first introduction to the TR7 Drophead was with the hood down on a sunny February day, which at once reminded one of the delights of open air motoring which can now be much better enjoyed in the winter due to the improvement in heaters. The heater unit gave excellent temperature control by means of an air blending regulator, with generous output and three-speed boost.

With the hood in place, the sealing was excellent and the interior as snug as the

closed coupe. Visibility all round was better than the fixed head TR7, thanks to the transparent panels in the rear three-quarter.

The driving position was acceptably comfortable, with the chubby steering wheel set at an ideal arm's length and with generous legroom and range of seat adjustment. At first the driving seat seemed a little uncomfortable, but it soon emerged that it was a matter of getting the back rest angle just right for maximum comfort. The seats had good lateral support, and extended well forward under the thighs. Small headrests were fitted to the seats for optimum restraint.

Well arranged minor controls, with the indicators and headlamp flash/dip lever on the left to meet international regulations were well suited for the driver. The instruments were very clearly marked, with slender white pointers on the large speedometer and rev counter. The minor instruments tended to be obscured by the wheel rim, but could be read if the driver moved his head slightly, to reveal fuel contents, coolant temperature, battery voltage and clock.

The interior trim of the TR7 was revised for the Drophead, with good imitation leather trim for the seat edges, gear lever gaiter and console. Seat centre panels were of a weaved cloth. The rather bulky looking facia panel might have been better styled, but it did include a sensibly large lockable facia compartment, and the panel tops were matt black to prevent windscreen reflections.

Minor switches in the centre included hazard warning, rear fog lamps, and main lighting switch. The rear fog lamp switch was fitted with two positions, to cope with the addition of front fog lamps. Turning the main light switch automatically raises the car's 'pop-up' headlamps. The lamps were also raised if the flasher switch was

The interior of the TR7 had traditional appeal in a more modern style

GENERAL SPECIFICATION

Engine
Head/block	alloy/cast iron
Cylinders	4 in line
Bore/stroke	90·3 × 78 mm
Capacity	1,998 cc
Cooling	water
Valve gear	ohc
Compression	9·29:1
Carburettor	twin SU HS6
Max. power	105 bhp at 5,000 rpm
Max. torque	119 lb-ft at 3,500 rpm

Transmission
Type	5-speed manual
Gear ratios and mph/1,000 rpm	
Top	0·83:1/20·8
4th	1·00:1/17·3
3rd	1·40:1/12·3
2nd	2·09:1/8·3
1st	3·32:1/5·2
Final drive	3·9:1

Suspension
Front	independent by coil springs, MacPherson struts, anti-roll bar
Rear	live axle, four link system, coil springs, anti-roll bar

Steering
Type	Alford & Adler rack and pinion
Assistance	no

Brakes
Front	Lockheed 9·75-in disc
Rear	Lockheed 9-in drum
Servo	yes

Wheels
Type	pressed steel
Tyres	185/70HR–13 in

Electrical
Battery	12v, 40 a-h
Earth	negative
Alternator	Lucas 17ACR, 36 amp

The 2-litre engine was based on the Dolomite power unit

PERFORMANCE DATA
Date of test 15th March 1980

Maximum speeds	mph	rpm
Top	114	5,450
4th	112	6,500
3rd	80	6,500
2nd	54	6,500
1st	34	6,500

Acceleration from rest	
mph	sec
0–30	3·0
0–40	5·0
0–50	7·1
0–60	10·7
0–70	14·2
0–80	19·8
0–90	27·1
0–100	42·0

Standing ¼ mile		18·1

Acceleration in	top	4th
mph	sec	sec
10–30	—	9·2
20–40	11·4	8·6
30–50	11·3	8·1
40–60	11·1	8·2
50–70	12·4	8·7
60–80	14·8	10·6
70–90	19·1	13·3
80–100	27·4	23·0

Fuel consumption	
Overall	25·3 mpg
Tank capacity	12 gal.
Max. range	300 miles

used, staying up for five seconds. The halogen headlights gave excellent range and dipped beam illumination without troubling on-coming drivers.

Two recessed levers secured the hood header rail to the top of the windscreen. Putting the hood up was straightforward, although it was a little difficult to engage the tongues at the top of the screen. The hood was easy enough to lower, but the arrangement was slightly spoiled by the all-too-common fault that the tonneau cover material fell short, leaving a fearful struggle to engage the press studs; it had to be pulled very tight to fasten properly.

For routine maintenance purposes, access to all components in the engine bay under the front-hinged bonnet was excellent.

Despite the acclaim of the TR7 Drophead, it was announced in May 1981 that production of the last mass-produced British sports car was to cease. Although the introduction in America of the TR8 – using the de-toxed Rover V8 engine – began to find a lot of appeal, BL was hard hit by the strength of Sterling against the US dollar and forced to choose between pricing themselves right out of the market or selling cars for less than it cost to make them. With the US market accounting for over 80 per cent of sales, the situation could not continue, and unfortunately production of the TR7 was terminated.

TVR Tasmin

The Blackpool based TVR company is a true survivor. Many of the small specialist 'kit-car' companies of the 1960s and 1970s are with us no more, killed off by VAT, Type Approval or even by a simple lack of business acumen. TVR had their fair share of problems, but in January 1980, after more than 20 years building sports cars, they faced the future with the striking Tasmin coupe.

The sleek body, designed by ex-Lotus man Oliver Winterbottom (where he was responsible for the Elite and Eclat), stuck to the TVR tradition, with a long nose and short stumpy tail. Good looks, of course, are not everything in a car, but in the TVR the appearance is not misleading, for the Tasmin has all the facets of a grand touring car – it is exhilarating for the driver and passenger as well as being an entirely practical and enjoyable long distance express.

The Tasmin uses proven running gear, and as production of the British Ford Essex 3-litre engine was tailing off, so TVR decided to fit the German Ford 2·8-litre engine from the outset, and chose the fuel injected version rated at 160 bhp (DIN) at 5,700 rpm. It is a V6 design with overhead pushrod valve gear, and Bosch K-Jetronic fuel injection. Cold start mixture adjustment is automatic, and in the magnificent way of most injection engines, it had the satisfying ability to fire up from cold and pulled strongly without any trace of snatch or hesitation.

Twin exhausts are fitted, and they emit a purposeful snarl under acceleration which goes well with the feeling of vitality and responsiveness pervading the car as a whole. There is smooth, vigorous response to the throttle when the driver uses the performance, coupled with docile, snatch-free running in top or third when trickling along in the traffic.

TVR use the standard Ford four-speed gearbox without overdrive or a fifth gear. The ratios are well spaced, and a good high first gear allows a smart getaway with 40 mph cleared before the first change is needed, 60 mph is seen in 8·2 sec and 100 mph in an impressive 23·2 sec. With its undeniably good aerodynamic shape, the Tasmin leads one to expect a high top speed, and the mean maximum of 130 mph does not disappoint. Maxima in the indirect gears are 44, 72 and 98 mph, and the top gear is still very much a performance gear – it is not always necessary on the open road to change down to third for overtaking.

The excellent Ford V6 2·8-litre power plant fills the engine bay

The quality interior has the rather small instruments in a lacquered burr walnut facia

The gearchange has a stubby short-travel lever protruding from the rather high tunnel between the seats. It offers rather more resistance to quick changes than one might expect after driving Fords with the same box. Clutch take-up is smooth with plenty of bite, and the driver can easily make a quick getaway when he needs to nip out into the traffic without any fear of stalling the engine.

An engine of nearly 3 litres in quite a heavy car of such character tempts everyone who drives it to put his or her foot down rather hard, and so one cannot expect too much in the way of economy. It is reasonable to look to 20 mph in general running with fast cruising and liberal use of the performance, improving to 24 mpg on a long trip if the car is not pushed too hard. The fuel tank holds 14 gallons giving a working range of 250 miles between fill-ups.

Like previous TVRs, the Tasmin has all-independent suspension, using wishbones and coil springs at the front, but the rear layout is substantially altered, using a long semi-trailing arm, a transverse link and fixed-length drive shafts. Telescopic dampers with concentric coil springs are fitted behind the drive shaft. The supension is very firm, as befits such a car, and produces quite a sharp jolt and taut vertical movement over bumps and undulations. However, this enhances the feeling of tautness and vitality that goes with the car as a whole, and there is no suggestion of wheel hop or sideways patter on poor and uneven road surfaces.

The TVR Tasmin epitomises the wedge-shaped styling of the 1980s

GENERAL SPECIFICATION

Engine
Head/block	cast iron
Cylinders	6 in vee
Bore/stroke	93 × 68·5 mm
Capacity	2,792 cc
Cooling	water
Valve gear	overhead pushrod
Compression	9·2:1
Injection	Bosch K-Jetronic
Max. power	160 bhp at 5,700 rpm
Max. torque	162 lb-ft at 4,300 rpm

Transmission
Type	4-speed manual
Gear ratios and mph/1,000 rpm	
Top	1·00:1/23·04
3rd	1·41:1/16·34
2nd	1·94:1/11·88
1st	3·16:1/7·29
Final drive	3·07:1

Suspension
Front	independent by coil springs, wishbones, anti-roll bar
Rear	independent by coil springs

Steering
Type	rack and pinion
Assistance	no

Brakes
Front	10·6-in disc
Rear	10·9-in disc
Servo	yes

Wheels
Type	alloy
Tyres	205/60VR–14 in

Electrical
Battery	12v, 60 a-h
Earth	negative
Alternator	55 amp
Headlamps	150/106W

On the road, the Tasmin set down squarely and firmly through a corner, with minimal roll and impressively well-balanced handling. There was no pronounced understeer to spoil it, but it was a little too readily provoked into a somewhat juddery rear breakaway. This happened forgivably enough except on the unpredictable occasions when, even with a nearly full tank, fuel leaked through a breather on to the outside tyre, caused an alarmingly sudden slide.

Steering is by rack and pinion, and there is no power assistance; the steering wheel is unusually small, being just over a foot in

The 'chopped' rear keeps up the TVR tradition.

diameter. The steering is fairly high geared and transmits a lot of wheel shock due to reactions on bumps and potholes.

Disc brakes are fitted all-round, with the ones at the front being inboard, and they are most reassuring for fast driving.

The Tasmin doors open wide, and getting in provides no real problem for anyone reasonably agile. Inside, the car feels snug yet spacious. The seats are upholstered in sude in the central wearing area, with ambla side pieces. Legroom is generous and there is good range of back rest adjustment. Once inside, the instruments – set in an attractive lacqured burr walnut facia panel – are visible through the steering wheel, but were rather small and difficult to read, especially at night.

Rear luggage space is quite good, although because of the coupe's rear glass panel there is no provision for concealing its contents from prying eyes. The spare wheel stands vertically at the rear of the compartment, located by sections of board with carpet attached.

High praise is deserved for the impeccable finish and neat fit of all the glassfibre bodywork. It is all first class workmanship, reflecting TVR's long experience in this material.

Since its introduction, TVR have extended the Tasmin range. At the Birmingham Motor Show in October 1980 they revealed the Tasmin convertible and the longer wheelbase 2+2 coupe versions, which together with the original two-seater coupe, were updated with flared wheel arches, sill skirts, a larger luggage platform and the option of automatic transmission. The Earls Court Motorfair one year later saw the debut of a 2-litre Ford-engined TVR with similar bodywork.

PERFORMANCE DATA
Date of test 2nd August 1980

Maximum speeds

	mph	rpm
Top	130	5,660
3rd	98	6,000
2nd	72	6,050
1st	44	6,000

Acceleration from rest

mph	sec
0–30	3·2
0–40	4·7
0–50	6·4
0–60	8·2
0–70	10·3
0–80	13·3
0–90	16·8
0–100	23·2
0–110	32·5

Standing ¼ mile 16·4

Acceleration in

mph	top sec	3rd sec
10–30	—	6·1
20–40	8·1	5·5
30–50	8·3	5·4
40–60	8·6	5·4
50–70	8·7	5·3
60–80	9·5	5·7
70–90	10·3	6·5
80–100	11·8	—
90–110	15·7	—

Fuel consumption
Overall 21·6 mpg
Tank capacity 14 gal.
Max. range 300 miles

Lotus Esprit Turbo

Lotus' decision to build more expensive and more sophisticated high performance sports cars led to the introduction of the Elite and the Eclat, effectively replacing the Elan. The move to the upper price bracket corresponded to the early 1970s oil crisis and the company's survival is a tribute to the cars they produce.

The introduction of the Giugioro-styled Lotus Esprit at the 1975 Paris Show was the final step in the Norfolk-based company's move 'up-market'. The Esprit replaced the mid-engined Europa, albeit at a considerably higher price.

Following the normal Lotus backbone chassis concept, the Esprit has unequal length double wishbone front suspension. At the rear it has a typically simple but effective set-up having the top transverse suspension link formed by a fixed-length driveshaft, while connected to the centre of the bottom of the rear upright is another transverse link. This, together with a fabricated semi-trailing arm also attached to the upright and running forward to a point on the backbone, forms a wide-based bottom 'wishbone'.

Autocar's initial verdict on the Lotus Esprit Series 2 in 1979 was that it was a noisy thoroughbred. When a company with such engineering (and engine) experience as Lotus decided to apply its talents to turbocharging the result was going to be something special. The Lotus Esprit Turbo is just that.

The Esprit Turbo was introduced in 1980, with a Garrett AiResearch T3 turbocharger bolted directly to a special exhaust manifold casting, on the all-alloy 2,174 cc engine. Like the normally aspirated 45 degree slant-four engine, the turbo unit (designated the 910) is significantly oversquare with a bore and stroke of 95·29 mm × 76·20 mm.

Special pistons lower the static compression ratio to 7·5-to-1, the exhaust valves are sodium cooled. Power is quoted at 210 bhp (DIN) from 6,000 to 6,500 rpm with

TVR Tasmin

The Blackpool based TVR company is a true survivor. Many of the small specialist 'kit-car' companies of the 1960s and 1970s are with us no more, killed off by VAT, Type Approval or even by a simple lack of business acumen. TVR had their fair share of problems, but in January 1980, after more than 20 years building sports cars, they faced the future with the striking Tasmin coupe.

The sleek body, designed by ex-Lotus man Oliver Winterbottom (where he was responsible for the Elite and Eclat), stuck to the TVR tradition, with a long nose and short stumpy tail. Good looks, of course, are not everything in a car, but in the TVR the appearance is not misleading, for the Tasmin has all the facets of a grand touring car – it is exhilarating for the driver and passenger as well as being an entirely practical and enjoyable long distance express.

The Tasmin uses proven running gear, and as production of the British Ford Essex 3-litre engine was tailing off, so TVR decided to fit the German Ford 2·8-litre engine from the outset, and chose the fuel injected version rated at 160 bhp (DIN) at 5,700 rpm. It is a V6 design with overhead pushrod valve gear, and Bosch K-Jetronic fuel injection. Cold start mixture adjustment is automatic, and in the magnificent way of most injection engines, it had the satisfying ability to fire up from cold and pulled strongly without any trace of snatch or hesitation.

Twin exhausts are fitted, and they emit a purposeful snarl under acceleration which goes well with the feeling of vitality and responsiveness pervading the car as a whole. There is smooth, vigorous response to the throttle when the driver uses the performance, coupled with docile, snatch-free running in top or third when trickling along in the traffic.

TVR use the standard Ford four-speed gearbox without overdrive or a fifth gear. The ratios are well spaced, and a good high first gear allows a smart getaway with 40 mph cleared before the first change is needed, 60 mph is seen in 8·2 sec and 100 mph in an impressive 23·2 sec. With its undeniably good aerodynamic shape, the Tasmin leads one to expect a high top speed, and the mean maximum of 130 mph does not disappoint. Maxima in the indirect gears are 44, 72 and 98 mph, and the top gear is still very much a performance gear – it is not always necessary on the open road to change down to third for overtaking.

The excellent Ford V6 2·8-litre power plant fills the engine bay

The quality interior has the rather small instruments in a lacquered burr walnut facia

The Esprit's aerodynamic shape is somewhat interrupted when the headlights are raised

200 lb-ft torque between 4,000 and 4,500 rpm. Perhaps more significant, there is more than 140 lb-ft (around the old Esprit's maximum) between 2,000 and 2,500 rpm!

Drive goes through a larger clutch to the normal five-speed Lotus/Citroen transaxle. Overall gearing is 22·7 mph per 1,000 rpm.

The most significant modifications on the Turbo from the earlier normally aspirated Esprits is the strengthened backbone chassis around the engine bay, divorcing the engine and transaxle from the suspension links and plunging driveshafts.

Goodyear ultra low profile NCT tyres (235/60 VR – 15 rears and 195/60VR – 15 fronts) are fitted on 7 in and 8 in wide rims respectively.

A number of aerodynamic modifications took place at the time of the Turbo's introduction to maintain aerodynamic balance, reduce lift, and provide the necessary extra engine bay cooling airflow. These include larger front and rear spoilers, side sills with NACA ducts to provide cooling air for the engine compartment, louvres for

The rather large lettering proclaiming the car's name is not to everyones' taste

Below: The winged instrument binnacle contained all the main instruments. The interior has a predominance of leather

Bottom: One of the problems of mid-engined sports cars: access to the engine is rather restricted

this air to exit through, and a deflector plate sited at the forward edge of the engine bay to encourage under-car airflow up through the engine bay.

The first thing a driver notices is the engine's extraordinary flexibility and the way it picks up from low rpm. Squeeze the throttle in second or third gears with as little as 1,500 rpm indicated and the engine pulls usefully and without complaint. At 2,000 rpm there is all the acceleration response one normally needs. Above 2,500 rpm the car surges forward yet without the big 'step' on to the power curve one normally associates with turbocharged engines. Certainly bottom end response has not been achieved at the expense of top end power. The engine revs with an almost eerie smoothness straight round to its 7,000 rpm limit (there is no red line). Maxima in well-spaced gears are 39, 62, 91 and 125 mph. Taking the car to the Continent

GENERAL SPECIFICATION

Engine
Head/block	alloy
Cylinders	4 in line, mid-mounted
Bore/stroke	95·29 × 76·20 mm
Capacity	2,174 cc
Cooling	water
Valve gear	twin ohc
Compression	7·5:1
Carburettor	2 Dellorto 40DHLA
Turbocharger	Garret AiResearch T3
Max. power	210 bhp at 6,000 rpm
Max. torque	200 lb-ft at 4,000 rpm

Transmission
Type	5-speed manual
Gear ratios and mph/1,000 rpm	
Top	0·76:1/22·7
4th	0·97:1/17·8
3rd	1·32:1/13·0
2nd	1·94:1/8·8
1st	2·92:1/5·9
Final drive	4·375:1

Suspension
Front	independent by coil springs, upper wishbone, lower transverse link, anti-roll bar
Rear	unequal length transverse links, radius arm, coil springs

Steering
Type	rack and pinion
Assistance	no

Brakes
Front	Girling 9·7-in disc
Rear	Girling 10·82-in disc
Servo	yes

Wheels
Type	alloy
Tyres—front	195/60VR–15 in
rear	235/60VR–15 in

Electrical
Battery	12v, 44 a-h
Earth	negative
Alternator	Lucas 18ACR
Headlamp	halogen 60/55W

PERFORMANCE DATA
Date of test 23rd May 1981

Maximum speeds	mph	rpm
Top	148	6,550
4th	125	7,000
3rd	91	7,000
2nd	62	7,000
1st	39	7,000

Acceleration from rest	
mph	sec
0–30	2·3
0–40	3·2
0–50	4·7
0–60	6·1
0–70	8·3
0–80	10·3
0–90	13·0
0–100	17·0
0–110	20·7
0–120	27·1
0–130	39·2

Standing ¼ mile   14·6

Acceleration in	top	4th
mph	sec	sec
20–40	14·9	8·3
30–50	10·4	5·8
40–60	8·3	5·4
50–70	8·5	5·5
60–80	8·4	5·4
70–90	8·7	5·7
80–100	9·2	6·2
90–110	10·5	7·6
100–120	13·1	10·6
110–130	19·3	—

Fuel consumption	
Overall	18 mpg
Tank capacity	19 gal.
Max. range	340 miles

Top: The Esprit has a deep front air dam

Above: The view most drivers see of this sports car

allowed *Autocar* to establish a mean maximum speed of 148 mph.

On the road this performance translates – mechanically at any rate – into a car that responds beautifully to small throttle openings in town, like a much larger normally aspirated unit, while on the open road there is simply a long flow of effortless power in each gear.

When testing, although unable to match Lotus' claims, the Esprit went well enough; to 30 mph in 2·3 sec as wheelspin (after a dumped clutch start with 5,000 rpm indicated) blended progressively into strong acceleration, to 60 mph in 6·1 sec (Lotus claim a shattering 5·5 sec), 100 mph in 17·0 sec, and 130 mph in 39·2 sec.

The gearchange is a little on the heavy side and rather indistinctly gated when making the dogleg from fourth to fifth, or when downchanging across the gate from third to second.

A manual choke is fitted and starting from cold is always immediate, followed by good driveability during a short warm up period. The engine is totally free of quirks, handling heavy traffic without fuss and always providing a delicious surge of acceleration when asked.

An overall fuel consumption figure of 18 mpg coupled to the twin fuel tanks that hold a total of 19 gallons gives the car a range of at least 340 miles before the fuel warning light glows, with 2 gallons remaining.

To enjoy the Esprit Turbo is to take it on a long cross-country trip when one can maintain astonishing average speeds simply by exploiting its grip, handling and acceleration, and not necessarily by going

The ducts in the side sills carry air to the engine bay

particularly fast. In town the car's width and poor three-quarter rear visibility tend to inhibit, yet almost every other respect of its road behaviour inspires confidence.

All Lotus' aerodynamic and chassis tuning work has clearly paid off, because at all speeds the Esprit Turbo gives the driver a feeling of limpet-like contact with the road. More important it maintains extraordinarily consistent balance throughout a wide speed range.

On dry roads and at cornering speeds that often seem a trifle ambitious at first, the car simply goes round with grip to spare. It does not roll much, it responds keenly to small steering inputs, and does not get put off line by bumps and undulations. In the dry the limit is rarely the car, but more often the forward visibility with which to exploit its grip safely. Steering loads build nicely in relation to cornering speeds giving the driver a sense of how much latent adhesion there is available; this, and the sideways force acting on the occupants are often the only indicators that one is cornering very fast indeed.

Lotus have done particularly well on ride quality in such a light, yet enormously shod car. At low speeds it is taut, yet the suspension is still working to cushion the occupants, and there is less than the expected degree of jiggliness over rippled surfaces – certainly less than one finds in a Porsche 924 Carrera. Long undulations and confused surfaces are beautifully absorbed, particularly when the car is being worked hard'.

As with any low slung, mid-engined car, one has to stoop and then 'thread' oneself into the cockpit. The leather seats have fixed back rests, and the steering wheel is not adjustable yet most drivers find themselves comfortable behind the wheel. Confined by the high and wide centre backbone on one side and the door on the other, the Esprit gives the driver a sense of snugness, of being at one with the machine.

Luggage space is often limited in a mid-engined car and the Esprit Turbo is no exception. Two or three squashy bags, plus perhaps a briefcase, can be accommodated in the cloth-lined zip-up compartment behind the engine bay. Oddment space within the car is also limited to a glove box and a bin mounted on the centre console, but this seems a small price to pay for such a sports car – a paragon of the turbocharged type.

The chassis and suspension modifications of the Turbo were adopted for the normally aspirated Esprit Series 3 which was introduced in 1981. The S3 also has the larger front and rear spoilers side sill and air ducts of the Turbo.